René Descartes

Discourse on the Method for Reasoning Well and for Seeking Truth in the Sciences

Translated by
Ian Johnston Vancouver
Island University
Nanaimo, BC
Canada

Richer Resources Publications
Arlington, Virginia
USA

Descartes
Discourse on the Method for Reasoning Well and for Seeking Truth in the Sciences

Copyright 2010, 2014
by Richer Resources Publications
All rights reserved

Cover art by Ian Crowe

Richer Resources Publicaions
1926 N. Woodrow Street
Arlington, Virginia 22207
or via our web site at
www.RicherResourcesPublications.com

Print:
ISBN   978-1-935238-75-1
Library of Congress Control Number 2010931375

eBook:
ISBN 978-1-935238-72-0

Published by Richer Resources Publications Arlington, Virginia
Printed in the United States of America

TABLE OF CONTENTS

Historical Note   4

Discourse on Method

[Preface]   5

Part One   5

Part Two   10

Part Three   17

Part Four   22

Part Five   27

Part Six   38

Some Brief Introductory Comments on Descartes' *Discourse*   49

Historical Note

René Descartes (1596-1650) published *Discourse on Method* in 1637 as part of a work containing sections on optics, geometry, and meteorology. The fourth section, the *Discourse*, outlined the basis for a new method of investigating knowledge. He later (in 1641) published a more detailed exploration of the philosophical basis for this new approach to knowledge in *Meditations on First Philosophy*.

DISCOURSE ON METHOD

If this discourse seems too long to be read in a single sitting, it can be divided up into six parts. In the first will be found various considerations concerning the sciences; in the second, the principal rules of the method which the author has discovered; in the third, some rules of morality which he has derived by this method; in the fourth, the reasons which enable him to establish the existence of God and of the human soul, which are the foundations of his metaphysics; in the fifth part, the order of questions in physics which he has looked into, and particularly the explanation for the movements of the heart and for some other difficulties which are part of medicine, including the difference which exists between our souls and those of animals; in the last part, some matters he believes necessary for further advances in research into nature, beyond where he has been, along with some reasons which have induced him to write.

PART ONE

The most widely shared thing in the world is good sense, for everyone thinks he is so well provided with it that even those who are the most difficult to satisfy in everything else do not usually desire to have more good sense than they have. In this matter it is not likely that everyone is mistaken. But this is rather a testimony to the fact that the power of judging well and distinguishing what is true from what is false, which is really what we call good sense or reason, is naturally equal in all men, and thus the diversity of our opinions does not arise because some people are more reasonable than others, but only because we conduct our thoughts by different routes and do not consider the same things. For it is not enough to have a good mind. The main thing is to apply it well. The greatest minds are capable of the greatest vices as well as the greatest virtues, and those who proceed only very slowly, if they always stay on the right road, are able to advance a great deal further than those who rush along and wander away from it.

As for myself, I have never presumed that my mind was anything more perfect than the ordinary mind. I have often even wished that I could have thoughts as quick, an imagination as clear and distinct, or a memory as ample or as actively involved as some other people. And I know of no qualities other than these which serve to perfect the mind. As far as reason, or sense, is concerned, given that it is the only thing which makes us human and distinguishes us from the animals, I like to believe that it is entirely complete in each person, following in this the common opinion of philosophers, who say that differences of more and less should occur only

5

between *accidental characteristics* and not at all between the *forms* or *natures* of *individuals* of the same *species*.[1]

But I will not hesitate to state that I think I have been very fortunate to have found myself since my early years on certain roads which have led me to considerations and maxims out of which I have created a method by which, it seems to me, I have a way of gradually increasing my knowledge, raising it little by little to the highest point which the mediocrity of my mind and the short length of my life can allow it to attain. For I have already harvested such fruit from this method that, even though, in judging myself, I always try to lean towards the side of distrust rather than to that of presumption and although, when I look with a philosopher's eye on the various actions and enterprises of all men, there are hardly any which do not seem to me vain and useless, I cannot help deriving extreme satisfaction from the progress which I think I have already made in my research into the truth and conceiving such hopes for the future that, if among the occupations of men, simply as men, there is one which is surely good and important, I venture to think it is the one I have chosen.

However, it could be the case that I am wrong and that perhaps what I have taken for gold and diamonds is only a little copper and glass. I know how much we are subject to making mistakes in what touches ourselves and also how much we should beware of the judgments of our friends when they are in our favour. But I will be only too happy to make known in this discourse what roads I have followed and to reveal my life in it, as if in a picture, so that each person can judge it. Learning from current reports the opinions people have of this discourse may be a new way of educating myself, something I will add to those which I habitually use.

Thus, my design here is not to teach the method which everyone should follow in order to reason well, but merely to reveal the way in which I have tried to conduct my own reasoning. Those who take it upon themselves to give precepts must consider themselves more skillful than those to whom they give them, and if they are missing the slightest thing, then they are culpable. But since I intend this text only as a history, or, if you prefer, a fable, in which, among some examples which you can imitate, you will, in addition, perhaps find several others which you will have reason not to follow, I hope that it will be useful to some people, without harming anyone, and that everyone will find my frankness agreeable.

---

[1]Accidental characteristics (or accidents) are secondary features which may vary from one individual to another (e.g., colour, size); forms and natures are the essential characteristics which define the species (e.g., reason in human beings).

I was nourished on literature from the time of my childhood. Because people persuaded me that through literature one could acquire a clear and assured understanding of everything useful in life, I had an intense desire to take it up. But as soon as I had completed that entire course of study at the end of which one was usually accepted into the rank of scholars, I changed my opinion completely. For I found myself burdened by so many doubts and errors that it seemed to me I had gained nothing by trying to instruct myself, other than the fact that I had increasingly discovered my own ignorance. Yet I had been in one of the most famous schools in Europe, a place where I thought there must be erudite men, if there were such people anywhere on earth.[1] I had learned everything which the others ers learned there, but still, not being happy with the sciences which we were being taught, I had gone through all the books which came into my hands dealing with those sciences which are considered the most curious and rare.[2] In addition, I knew how other people were judging me, and I saw that they did not consider me inferior to my fellow students, although among them there were already some destined to fill the places of our teachers. And finally our age seemed to me as flourishing and as fertile in good minds as any preceding age. Hence, I took the liberty of judging all the others by myself and of thinking that there was no doctrine in the world of the kind I had previously been led to hope for.

However, I did not cease valuing the exercises which kept people busy in the schools. I knew that the languages one learns there are necessary for an understanding of ancient books, that the gracefulness of fables awakens the intellect, that the memorable actions of history raise the mind, and if one reads with discretion, help to form one's judgment, that reading all the good books is like a conversation with the most honourable people of past centuries, who were their authors, even a carefully prepared dialogue in which they reveal to us only the best of their thoughts, that eloquence has incomparable power and beauty, that poetry has a most ravishing delicacy and softness, that mathematics has very skillful inventions which can go a long way toward satisfying the curious as well as facilitating all the arts and lessening the work of men, that the writings which deal with morals contain several lessons and a number of exhortations to virtue which are extremely useful, that theology teaches one how to reach heaven, that philosophy provides a way of speaking plausibly on all matters and making oneself admired by those who are less scholarly, that jurisprudence, medicine, and the other sciences bring honour and riches to

---

[1] Descartes was educated at the Jesuit college of La Flèche for eight years.

[2] The word "science" in Descartes' vocabulary refers to any formally organized theoretical knowledge. Its meaning is not confined to natural science.

those who cultivate them, and finally that it is good to have examined all of them, even the most superstitious and false, in order to know their legitimate value and to guard against being wrong. But I believed I had already given enough time to languages and even to reading ancient books as well, and to their histories and stories. For talking with those from other ages is almost the same as travelling. It is good to know something about the customs of various people, so that we can judge our own more sensibly and do not think everything different from our own ways ridiculous and irrational, as those who have seen nothing are accustomed to do. But when one spends too much time travelling, one finally becomes a stranger in one's own country, and when one is too curious about things which went on in past ages, one usually lives in considerable ignorance about what goes on in this one. In addition, fables make us imagine several totally impossible events as possible, and even the most faithful histories, if they neither change nor increase the importance of things to make them more worth reading, at the very least almost always omit the most menial and less admirable circumstances, with the result that what is left in does not depict the truth. Hence, those who regulate their habits by the examples which they derive from these histories are prone to fall into the extravagances of the knights of our romances and to dream up projects which exceed their powers.

I placed a great value on eloquence, and I was in love with poetry, but I thought that both of them were gifts given to the mind rather than fruits of study. Those who have the most powerful reasoning and who direct their thoughts best in order to make them clear and intelligible can always convince us best of what they are proposing, even if they speak only the language of Lower Brittany and have never learned rhetoric. And those who possess the most pleasant creative talents and who know how to express them with the most adornment and smoothness cannot help being the best poets, even though the art of poetry is unknown to them.

I found mathematics especially delightful because of the certainty and clarity of its reasoning. But I did not yet notice its true use. Thinking that it was practical only in the mechanical arts, I was astonished that on its foundations, so strong and solid, nothing more imposing had been built up. By contrast, I compared the writings of the ancient pagans which deal with morality to really superb and magnificent palaces built on nothing but sand and mud. They raise the virtues to a very great height and make them appear valuable, above everything in the world, but they do not teach us to know them well enough, and often what they call by such a beautiful name is only apathy or pride or despair or parricide.[1]

I revered our theology and aspired as much as anyone to reach heaven, but having learned, as something very certain, that the road there is no less open to the most ignorant as to the most learned and that the revealed truths which lead there are beyond our intelligence, I did not dare to submit them to the frailty of my reasoning, and I thought that undertaking to examine them successfully would require me to have some extraordinary heavenly assistance and to be more than a man.

I will say nothing of philosophy other than this: once I saw that it had been cultivated for several centuries by the most excellent minds which had ever lived, and that, nonetheless, there was still nothing in it which was not disputed and which was thus not still in doubt, I did not have sufficient presumption to hope to fare better there than the others. Considering how many different opinions, maintained by learned people, philosophy could have about the same matter, without there ever being more than one which could be true, I reckoned as virtually false all those which were merely probable.

Then, as for the other sciences, since they borrow their principles from philosophy, I judged that nothing solid could have been built on such insubstantial foundations, and neither the honour nor the profit which they promise were sufficient to convince me to learn them, for, thank God, I did not feel myself in a condition which obliged me to make a profession of science in order improve my fortune, and, although I did not, in some cynical way, undertake to proclaim my disdain for glory, nonetheless I placed very little value on the fame I could hope to acquire only through false titles. And finally, as for bad doctrines, I thought I already understood sufficiently what they were worth in order not be taken in either by the promises of an alchemist, by the predictions of an astrologer, by the impostures of a magician, or by the artifice or the bragging of any of those who made a profession of knowing more than they know.

That is why, as soon as my age permitted me to leave the supervision of my professors, I completely stopped the study of letters, and, resolving not to look any more in any other science except one which could be found inside myself or in the great book of the world, I spent the rest of my youth travelling, looking into courts and armies, associating with people

---

[1]The word "parricide" may seem odd here, but it refers to acts committed against one's own family in the name of justice (i.e., a love of justice so strong that one is willing to kill members of one's own family who have done wrong). With certain pagan moralists (e.g., the Stoics), such acts were considered particularly virtuous.

of various humours and conditions, collecting various experiences, testing myself in the encounters which fortune offered me, and everywhere reflecting on the things I came across in such a way that I could draw some profit from them. For it seemed to me that I could arrive at considerably more truth in the reasoning that each man makes concerning the matters which are important to him and in which events could punish him soon afterwards if he judged badly, than in the reasoning made by a man of letters in his study concerning speculations which produce no effect and which are of no consequence to him, except perhaps that from them he can augment his vanity—and all the more so, the further his speculations are from common sense, because he would have had to use that much more wit and artifice in the attempt to make them probable. And I always had an extreme desire to learn to distinguish the true from the false, in order to see clearly in my actions and to proceed with confidence in this life.

It is true that while I did nothing but examine the customs of other men, I found hardly anything there to reassure me, and I noticed as much diversity among men as I had earlier among the opinions of philosophers. Consequently, the greatest profit which I derived from this was that, by seeing several things which, although they seem really extravagant and ridiculous to us, were commonly accepted and approved by other great people, I learned not to believe too firmly in anything which I had been persuaded to believe merely by example and by custom. Thus, I gradually freed myself of plenty of errors which can obfuscate our natural light and make us less capable of listening to reason. But after I had spent a few years studying in this way in the book of the world, attempting to acquire some experience, one day I resolved to study myself as well and to use all the powers of my mind to select paths which I should follow, a task which brought me considerably more success, it seems to me, than if I had never gone away from my own country and my books.

PART TWO

I was then in Germany, summoned by the wars which have not yet concluded there.[1] As I was returning to the army from the coronation of the emperor, the onset of winter stopped me in a place where, not finding any conversation to divert me and in addition, by good fortune, not having any

[1]In 1618 Descartes, who was Catholic, voluntarily joined the Protestant army of Maurice of Nassau, who was active in organizing the forces of the Dutch Republic in its fight with Spain. Shortly afterwards (in 1619) Descartes left the Netherlands and joined the Catholic armies of Maximillian, Duke of Bavaria. In 1620 he was present at the Battle of White Mountain in Prague, where the Czech Protestants were decisively beaten.

cares or passions to trouble me, I spent the entire day closed up alone in a room heated by a stove, where I had complete leisure to talk to myself about my thoughts. Among these, one of the first was that I noticed myself thinking about how often there is not so much perfection in works created from several pieces and made by the hands of various masters as there is in those which one person has worked on alone. Thus, we see that the buildings which a single architect has undertaken and completed are usually more beautiful and better ordered than those which several people have tried to refurbish by making use of old walls built for other purposes. That is why those ancient cities which were only small villages at the start and became large towns over time are ordinarily so badly laid out, compared to the regular places which an engineer has designed freely on level ground. Even though, considering the buildings in each of them separately, we often find as much beauty in the former town as in the latter, or more, nonetheless, looking at them as they are arranged—here a large one, there a small one—and the way they make the streets crooked and unequal, we would say that chance rather than the will of some men using their reason designed them this way. And if one considers that nonetheless there have always been certain officials charged with seeing that private buildings serve as a public ornament, one will readily see that it is difficult to achieve really fine things by working only with other people's pieces. Thus, I imagined to myself that people who were semi-savages in earlier times and who became civilized only little by little and created their laws only as they were compelled to by the extent to which crimes and quarrels bothered them would not be so well regulated as those who, from the moment they first assembled, followed the constitution of some prudent legislator. It is indeed certain that the state of the true religion, whose laws God alone created, must be incomparably better ordered than all the others. And, to speak of human affairs, I believe that if Sparta was in earlier times very prosperous, that was not on account of the goodness of each of its laws in particular, seeing that several were very strange and even contrary to good morals, but on account of the fact that they were devised by only a single man and thus they contributed towards the same end. Similarly I thought that the sciences contained in books, at least those whose reasons are only probable and without any proofs, since they were put together and crudely fashioned little by little out of the opinions of several different people, therefore did not approach the truth as much as the simple reasoning which a man of good sense can make quite naturally concerning matters of his own experience. In the same way I thought that because we were all children before we were men and because it was necessary for us to be governed for a long time by our appetites and our supervisors, who were often at odds with each other, with neither of them perhaps advising us always for the best, it is almost impossible that our judgments are as pure and solid as they would have been if we had had the total use of our reason from the moment of our birth and had never been led by anything but our reason.

It is true that we see little point in demolishing all the houses of a city for the sole purpose of rebuilding them in another way and thus making the streets more beautiful. But we do see several people demolish their houses in order to rebuild them, and, indeed, sometimes they are compelled to do so, when the houses are in danger of collapsing on their own and when their foundations are not steady. This example persuaded me that there would probably be little point for a particular man to draw up a design for reforming a state, changing all of it from the foundations, overturning it in order to put it up again, or even for reforming the body of sciences or the order established in the schools for teaching the sciences. But so far as all the opinions which I had received up to that point and which I believed credible were concerned, I convinced myself that the best possible thing for me to do was to undertake to remove them once and for all, so that afterwards I could replace them either by other better ones or perhaps by the same ones, once I had adjusted them to a reasonable standard. And I firmly believed that by this means I would be successful in conducting my life much better than if I built only on the old foundations and relied only on principles which I had been persuaded to accept in my youth, without ever having examined whether they were true. For, although I recognized various problems with this approach, these were not without remedy and could not compare to those which occur in the reform of the least matters concerning the public. It is too difficult to re-erect those large bodies if they are thrown down or even to keep them once they are weakened, and their collapses cannot be anything but very drastic. Then, as far as the imperfections of large public bodies are concerned, if they have any (and the variety among such bodies alone is sufficient to assure us that there are several imperfections), habit has no doubt considerably softened these and has even managed to avoid some problems or corrected a number of them insensibly, which people's caution could not have managed so well, and finally the imperfections are almost always easier to bear than changing them would be, in the same way that the major roads which wind among the mountains gradually become so smooth and convenient from being used, that it is much better to follow them than to set out to go more directly by climbing up over the rocks and going down right to the bottom of the precipices.

That is why I cannot approve at all of those muddled and worried temperaments who, without being summoned by their birth or fortune to the management of public business, never stop proposing some idea for a new reform in it. If I thought that there was the slightest thing in this text which would enable someone to suspect me of this foolishness, I would be very reluctant to allow it to be published. My intention has never been to do more than try to reform my own thoughts and to build on a foundation which is entirely my own. And if my work has pleased me sufficiently to make me show you the model of it here, that is not because I wish to advise anyone to imitate it. Those to whom God has given more of his grace will perhaps have loftier intentions, but I fear that this work may already be too bold for several people. The single resolution to strip away all the opinions which one has previously absorbed into one's beliefs is not an example which everyone should follow. Most of the world is made up of two sorts of minds for whom such a resolution is not suitable. First, there are those who, believing themselves more clever than they are, cannot stop making hasty judgments, without having enough patience to conduct their thoughts in an orderly way, with the result that, once they have taken the liberty of doubting the principles they have received and of leaving the common road, they will never be able to hold to the track which they need to take in order to proceed more directly and will remain lost all their lives. Then there are the ones who, having sufficient reason or modesty to judge that they are less capable of differentiating truth and falsehood than several others from whom they can be instructed, must content themselves with following the opinions of these others rather than searching for better opinions on their own.

As for me, I would have undoubtedly been among the number of this latter group if I had only had a single master or if I had known nothing at all about the differences which have always existed among the opinions of the most highly educated men. But I learned from my college days on that one cannot imagine anything so strange and so incredible that it has not been said by some philosopher and, later, in my travelling, I found out that all those who have views very different from our own are not therefore barbarians or savages, but that several use as much reason as we do, or more. I also considered how much the same man, with the same mind, raised from his infancy on among the French or the Germans, would become different from what he would have been if he had always lived among the Chinese or the cannibals, and how, even in our style of dress the same thing which pleased us ten years ago and which will perhaps please us again ten years from today, now seems to us extravagant and ridiculous. This being the case, we are clearly persuaded more by custom and example than by any certain knowledge. Nonetheless, a plurality of voices is not a proof worth anything for truths which are a little difficult to discover, because it is far more probable that one man by himself would have found them than an entire people. Since I could not select anyone whose opinions it seemed to me one should prefer to those of other people, I found myself, so to speak, compelled to guide myself on my own.

But like a man who proceeds alone and in the shadows, I resolved to go so slowly and to use so much circumspection in all matters, that if I only advanced a very short distance, at least I would take good care not to fall. I did not even wish to begin by rejecting completely any of the opinions which could have slipped into my beliefs previously without being introduced by reason, before I had taken up enough time drawing up a plan for the work I was undertaking and seeking out the true method for arriving at an understanding of everything my mind was capable of knowing.

When I was younger, among the branches of philosophy, I had studied a little logic and, among the subjects of mathematics, geometrical analysis and algebra, three arts or sciences which looked as if they ought to contribute something to my project. But in looking at them, I took care, because, so far as logic is concerned, its syllogisms and most of its other instructions serve to explain to others what one already knows or even, as in the art of Lully, to speak without judgment of things about which one is ignorant, rather than to learn what they are.[1] Although philosophy does, in in fact, contain many really true and excellent precepts, mixed in with them there are always so many injurious or superfluous ones that it is almost as difficult to separate them as to draw a Diana or a Minerva out of a block of marble which has not yet been carved. Then, so far as the analysis of the ancients and the algebra of the moderns are concerned, other than the fact that they deal only with really abstract matters, which have no apparent use, the former is always so concentrated on considering numbers that it cannot exercise the understanding without considerably tiring the imagination, and in the latter is so subject to certain rules and symbols that it has been turned into a confused and obscure art which clutters up the mind rather than a science which cultivates it. Those were the reasons why I thought I had to look for some other method which included the advantages of these three subjects but was free of their defects. And since a multitude of laws often provides excuses for vices, so that a state is much better ruled when it has only a very few laws which are very strictly observed, I thought that, instead of that large number of rules which make up logic, I would have enough with the four following rules, provided that I maintained a strong and constant resolution that I would never fail to observe them, not even once.

The first rule was that I would not accept anything as true which I did not clearly know to be true. That is to say, I would carefully avoid being over hasty or prejudiced, and I would understand nothing by my judgments beyond what presented itself so clearly and distinctly to my mind that I had no occasion to doubt it.

---

[1]Ramon Llull was a thirteenth-century philosopher who wrote a rational defence of Christianity.

The second was to divide each difficulty which I examined into as many parts as possible and as might be necessary to resolve it better.

The third was to conduct my thoughts in an orderly way, beginning with the simplest objects, the ones easiest to know, so that little by little I could gradually climb right up to the knowledge of the most complex, by assuming the same order, even among those things which do not naturally come one after the other.

And the last was to make my calculations throughout so complete and my review so general that I would be confident of not omitting anything.

Those long chains of reasons, all simple and easy, which geometers have habitually used to reach their most difficult proofs gave me occasion to imagine to myself that everything which could fall under human knowledge would follow in the same way and that, provided only that one refused to accept anything as true which was not and that one always kept to the order necessary to deduce one thing from another, there could not be anything so far distant that one could not finally reach it, nor so hidden that one could not discover it. And I did not have much trouble finding out the issues which I had to deal with first. For I already knew that it had to be with the simplest things, the ones easiest to know. When I thought about how, among all those who had so far searched for truth in the sciences, it was only the mathematicians who had been able to find some proofs, that is to say, some certain and evident reasons, I had no doubt at all that I should start with the same things which they had examined, although I did not hope for any practical results, other than that they would accustom my mind to revelling in the truth and not remaining happy with false reasons. But for all that I did not plan trying to learn all the particular sciences which people commonly call mathematical. Since I saw that, even though their objects were different, they were alike in that they all agreed they should consider nothing except the various relationships or proportions among the objects of study found there, I thought that it would be more valuable if I examined only these proportions in general, without assuming that they were present in the objects, except for those which would help to provide me knowledge of them most readily, but without in this way restricting them at all to those objects, so that they could be all the better applied later to every other object for which they might be suitable. Then, because I observed that, in order to understand these things, I would sometimes need to consider each one in particular and sometimes only to remember them or to understand several of them together, I thought that to consider them better separately, I ought to assume that they were like lines, because I know of nothing simpler, nothing which I could more distinctly represent to my imagination and my senses. But in order to remember them or to understand several of them together, I had to explain them by some formulas as short as possible and, by this means, I would borrow all the best elements of analytic geometry and algebra and would correct all the defects of one by the other.[1]

As a matter of fact, I venture to say that the precise observation of these few precepts which I had selected gave me such a facility at disentangling all the questions which these two sciences cover, that in the two or three months that I used them to examine these questions, starting with the simplest and the most general and letting each truth I found serve as a rule which I could use afterwards to find others, not only did I resolve several problems which I had previously judged very difficult, but it also seemed to me towards the end that I could determine, even with those questions where I was ignorant, the way to resolve them and the extent to which such resolution was possible. In saying this, perhaps I will not appear too vain if you consider that, since there is only one truth for each thing, whoever finds it knows as much as one can know about it and that, for example, a child instructed in arithmetic, having made an addition following the rules, can be confident of having found, so far as the sum he is examining is concerned, everything that the human mind can find out. For the method which teaches one to follow the true order and to count exactly all the relevant details in what one is looking for contains everything which gives certainty to the rules of arithmetic.

But what pleased me the most with this method was that with it I was confident of using all my reason, if not perfectly, at least as well as was in my power. In addition, I felt, as I applied it, that my mind was accustoming itself gradually to think more clearly and distinctly about its objects, and because I had not restricted this method to one matter in particular, I was hopeful that I could apply it just as usefully to difficulties in the other sciences as I had applied it to those in algebra. But for all that, I did not venture to try immediately examining all those scientific problems which presented themselves. For that would have been contrary to the order which my method prescribed. But I noticed that the principles of science all had to be borrowed from philosophy, a subject in which I no longer found anything certain. So I thought that, before anything else, I should attempt to establish such principles there and that, since this was the most important matter in the world, where one had to be most fearful of overhasty and biased judgments, I would not try to get through it until I had reached an age considerably more mature than I was then at twenty-three and until I had used a lot more time preparing myself, weeding out of my mind all the bad opinions which I had accepted before that time, as

---

[1]Descartes here is referring to his pioneering and celebrated work in analytic geometry, in which algebraic equations and the relationships they describe are represented geometrically.

well as collecting several experiences so that later they could be the subject matter of my reasoning, always practising the method which I had set for myself in order to keep on improving myself in these matters.

PART THREE

Finally, before one starts to rebuild the lodgings where one lives, it is not sufficient to knock them down and provide for materials and architects or to work on the architecture oneself, having, in addition to that, carefully drawn up a design. One must also provide oneself with some other place where one can lodge comfortably during the time one works on the building. Thus, in order not to be irresolute in my actions while my reason obliged me to be so in my judgments and in order not to prevent myself living from then on as happily as I could, I drew up for myself a provisional morality, consisting of only three or four maxims, which I wish to share with you.

The first was to obey the laws and the customs of my country, constantly holding to the religion which God gave me the grace to be instructed in since my childhood and governing myself in all other things in accordance with the most moderate opinions, the ones furthest removed from excess, which were commonly accepted and practised by the most sensible of those people among whom I would be living. Since, from that point on, I began to estimate my own views as worthless, because I wished to subject them all to examination, I was confident that I could not do better than to follow those of the most sensible people. And even though there might perhaps be people just as sensible among the Persians or the Chinese as among us, it seemed to me that the most practical thing would be for me to guide myself by those among whom I had to live and that, in order to understand their real opinions, it would be better for me to pay attention to what they practised rather than to what they said, not only because, given the corruption of our morals, there are few people who are willing to state everything they believe, but also because several are themselves ignorant of what they believe. For the act of thinking by which one believes in something is different from the act of thinking by which one understands that one believes it, and one of these separate acts frequently appears without the other. Moreover, among several opinions equally well received, I chose only the most moderate ones, as much because such opinions are always the most convenient to practice and probably the best, for all excess is usually bad, as because they would also not take me as far from the true road, if I made a mistake, as if I had chosen one of the extremes when it was the other one which I should have followed. And I especially included among what was excessive all promises by which one reduces one's liberty. Not that I disapprove of laws which, in an attempt to remedy the fickleness of feeble minds, permit people with a good plan or even an indifferent arrangement for security in business to make vows or contracts obliging them to maintain their provisions. But because I did not see anything in the world which remained always in the same condition and, in my particular case, because I promised myself that I would increasingly perfect my judgments and not make them worse, I would have thought I was committing a great error in good sense if, because I then approved of something, I obliged myself to continue to take it as something good later on, when it had perhaps ceased to be so or when I had ceased to value it as something good.

My second maxim was to be as constant and as resolute in my actions as I could, and to follow the most doubtful opinions, once I had settled on them for myself, with no less constancy than if they had been very sure, imitating in this matter travellers who, finding themselves lost in some forest, should not wander around, shifting direction this way and that; even less should they stop in one place; they should move on always as straight as they can in the same direction and not change it for inadequate reasons, even though at the beginning it was perhaps only chance which led to their choice of direction. For in this way, if they do not come out exactly where they want to, they will at least end up arriving somewhere where they will probably be better off than in the middle of a forest. And because the actions of life often brook no delay, it is certainly very true that, when it is not in our power to determine the truest opinions, we ought to follow the most probable ones, and even when we see no difference in probability among this group of truths or that one, nevertheless, we have to decide on some for ourselves and then to consider them, not as something doubtful with regard to the practical matter at hand, but as manifestly true and very certain, because the reason which made us choose them has these qualities. This method was able from then on to relieve me of all the regrets and remorse which usually upset the consciences of those weak and wavering minds which permit themselves to work inconsistently with things which they accept as good but which they later judge to be bad.

My third maxim was to try always to overcome myself rather than fortune and to change my desires rather than the order of the world, and generally to get in the habit of believing that there is nothing which is entirely within our power except our thoughts, so that after we have done our best concerning those things which lie outside of us, everything which our attempt fails to deal with is, so far as we are concerned, absolutely impossible. That alone seemed to me to be sufficient to prevent me from desiring anything in future which I might not achieve and thus to make me happy. For since our will has a natural tendency to desire only things which our understanding represents as in some way possible, it is certain that if we think about all the good things which are outside of us as equally distant from our power, we would no more regret missing those whose loss appears due to our birth, when we are deprived by no fault of our own, than we would regret not possessing the kingdoms of China or Mexico. By making, as the saying goes, a virtue of necessity, we would not desire health when we are sick or freedom when we are in prison, any more than we now desire to have either a body made of some material as incorruptible as diamonds or wings to fly, like the birds. But I admit that there is a need for a long discipline and frequently repeated meditation in order to accustom oneself to looking at everything from this point of view. And I believe that this is the principal secret of those philosophers who have been able in earlier times to escape from the demands of empire and fortune and who, despite pains and poverty, could rival their gods in happiness. For, constantly busy thinking about the limits prescribed for them by nature, they persuaded themselves so perfectly that nothing was in their power except their thoughts, that that alone would be enough to prevent them from having any affection for other things, and they acquired such an absolute control over their thoughts that they found in that process reason to think themselves more rich and more powerful and more free and more content than any other men, who, because they did not possess this philosophy, never had the same control over everything they desired, no matter how favoured they might be by nature and fortune.

Finally, to conclude these moral precepts, I advised myself to draw up a review of the various occupations which men have in this life, in an attempt to make a choice about the best and, without wanting to say anything about the others, I thought that I could not do better than to continue in the very occupation I was engaged in, that is, using all my life to cultivate my reason and to progress as far as I could in a knowledge of the truth, following the method which I had prescribed for myself. I experienced such extreme contentment once I started using this method that I did not think that one could find anything more sweet and innocent in this life. Since every day I discovered through this method some truths which seemed to me sufficiently important and commonly unknown to other men, the satisfaction I got from it so filled my mind that nothing else affected me. Moreover, the three maxims mentioned above were founded only for the plan I had to continue my self-instruction. For since God has given each one of us some light to distinguish truth from falsehood, I would not have thought I could remain content with other people's opinions for one moment, if I had not set out to use my own judgment to examine them when the time was right, and I would not have known how to free myself from scruples in following these opinions, if I had not hoped that I would not, in the process, lose any opportunity to find better ones, in cases where these existed. Finally I would not have known how to limit my desires nor how to rest content, if I had not followed a road by which I believed I could be confident of acquiring all the knowledge I was capable of. I thought by the same means I could acquire all the true benefits I was capable of obtaining, all the more so since our will tends to follow or to fly away from only those things which our understanding has represented to it as good or bad. So in order to act well it is sufficient to judge well, and to judge as well as one can is sufficient to enable one to do one's best, that is, to acquire all the virtues, along with all the other benefits which one can get, and when one is certain that that is the case one could not fail to be content.

After assuring myself of these maxims in this manner and storing them away, along with the truths of the faith, which have always been first in my beliefs, I judged that, so far as all the rest of my opinions were concerned, I could freely set about dispensing with them. Since I hoped to be able to arrive at my goal more easily by talking with men rather than staying any longer closed up in the room with the stove where I had had all these thoughts, before that winter was over and done with, I set about my travels again. And in all the nine years following I did nothing else but roll around here and there in the world, trying to be a spectator rather than an actor in all the comedies playing themselves out there. By reflecting on each matter, in particular on what there was which could render it suspect and give us an opportunity to make mistakes, I rooted out from my mind all the errors which could have slid into it in the previous years. Not that in the process I copied the skeptics, who doubt only for the sake of doubting, and pretend that they are always irresolute. For my entire plan, by contrast, tended only to make me confident about throwing away the shifting ground and the sand, in order to find the rock or the sedimentary clay. This gave me considerable success, it seems to me, inasmuch as in my attempts to discover the falsity or the uncertainty of the propositions I examined, not by weak conjectures, but by clear and confident reasoning, I came across nothing so doubtful that I did not always draw some fairly certain conclusion from it, even if that conclusion was that it contained nothing certain. Just as when we tear down an old lodging, we usually keep the scrap to use in building a new structure, so, as I destroyed all those opinions of mine which I judged poorly grounded, I made various observations and acquired several experiences which were of use to me later in establishing more certain ones. In addition, I continued to practice the method which I had set for myself. For apart from the fact that I took care, in general, to conduct all my thinking according to the rules, from time to time I set aside a few hours which I used to apply the method to mathematical difficulties in particular, or even to some other difficulties as well, ones which I could frame in a manner somewhat similar to those in mathematics, stripping from them all the principles of the other sciences which I did not find sufficiently strong, as you will see I have done in several which are explained in this volume.[1] Thus, without living in a way apparently different from those who have nothing else to do but spend a sweet and innocent life studying how to separate pleasures from vices and enjoying their leisure by making use of all honourable entertainments without getting bored, I did not fail to follow my plans and to benefit from the knowledge of the truth, perhaps more so than if I had only read books or associated with men of letters.

However, these nine years passed by before I had yet taken any stand concerning the difficulties which are usually matters of dispute among the scholars. Nor had I started to seek the foundations of any philosophy more reliable than common philosophy. The example of several excellent minds who had earlier had the same idea but who, it seemed to me, had not succeeded, made me imagine such great difficulties that I would perhaps not have ventured to undertake it so quickly, if I had not seen that some people had already spread the rumour that I had concluded my work. I don't know what to say about the basis for this rumour. And if I contributed something to it by my conversations, that could have been by confessing where I was ignorant more ingenuously than those who have studied little are accustomed to do and perhaps also by making known the reasons I had to doubt many things which other people considered certain, rather than by boasting about any doctrine. But having a heart sufficiently good not to wish people to take me for someone other than the man I am, I thought it necessary to attempt by every means to make myself worthy of the reputation which people ascribed to me. For exactly eight years this desire made me resolve to distance myself from all those places where there might be people I know and to retire here, in a country where the long duration of the war has established such order that the armies which maintain it appear to serve only to enable the people to enjoy the fruits of peace with even more security and where, among the crowd of a great and very active people, who are more careful about their own affairs than curious about those of other people, with no lack of any commodities present in the most frequently visited towns, I was able to live retired in solitude, just as if I were in the most isolated deserts.[2]

PART FOUR

I don't know if I should share with you the first meditations which I made there, for they are so metaphysical and so out of the ordinary that they will perhaps not be to everyone's taste. However, in order that people may

---

[1]In the same book as this *Discourse*, Descartes included sections on optics, geometry, and meteorology.

[2]That is, in Holland. The "nine years" Descartes refers to earlier are 1619-1628.

be able to judge if the foundations which I set are sufficiently strong, I find myself in some way compelled to speak of them. For a long time previously I had noticed that where morals are concerned it is necessary sometimes to follow opinions which one knows are extremely uncertain as if they are indubitable, as mentioned above. But since at that time I wanted only to carry out research into the truth, I thought I must do the opposite and reject as absolutely false everything about which I could imagine the least doubt, in order to see if there would be anything totally indisputable remaining after that in my belief. Thus, because our senses deceive us sometimes, I was willing to assume that there was nothing which existed the way our senses present it to us. And because there are men who make mistakes in reasoning, even concerning the most simple matters of geometry, and who create paralogisms, and because I judged that I was subject to error just as much as anyone else, I rejected as false all the reasons which I had taken earlier as proofs. Finally, considering that all the same thoughts which we have when awake can also come to us when we are asleep, without there being truth in any of them at the time, I determined to pretend that everything which had ever entered my mind was no more true than the illusions of my dreams. But immediately afterwards I noticed that, while I wished in this way to think everything was false, it was necessary that I—who was doing the thinking—had to be something. Noticing that this truth—*I think; therefore, I am*—was so firm and so sure that all the most extravagant assumptions of the skeptics would not be able to weaken it, I judged that I could accept it without scruple as the first principle of the philosophy I was looking for.[1]

Then I examined with attention what I was, and I saw that I could pretend that I had no body and that the world and the place where I was did not exist, but that, in spite of this, I could not pretend that I did not exist. By contrast, in the very act of thinking about doubting the truth of other things, it very clearly and certainly followed that I existed; whereas, if I had only stopped thinking, even though all the other things which I had ever imagined were real, I would have no reason to believe that I existed. From that I recognized that I was a substance whose essence or nature is only thinking, a substance which has no need of any location and does not

---

[1] In the Latin of Descartes' *Meditations*, which provides a fuller discussion of his reasoning about these vital first principles, this statement "I think; therefore, I am" (*je pense, donc je suis*) is the famous statement *Cogito ergo sum*. As the subsequent lines in the discussion above indicate, this claim might be more properly translated "I am thinking; therefore, I am," since the certainty remains only during the process of thinking. Descartes is here simply summarizing the process he went through in reaching this famous conclusion. Those who are interested in looking at the argument and at objections to it in more detail should read his *Meditations*.

depend on any material thing, so that this "I," that is to say, the soul, by which I am what I am, is entirely distinct from the body and is even easier to know than the body, and that, even if the body were no longer there, the soul could not help being everything it is.

After that, I considered in general what is necessary for a proposition to be true and certain, for since I had just found one idea which I knew to be true and certain, I thought that I ought also to understand what this certitude consisted of. And having noticed that in the sentence "I think; therefore, I am" there is nothing at all to assure me that I am speaking the truth, other than that I see very clearly that in order to think it is necessary to exist, I judged that I could take as a general rule the point that the things which we conceive very clearly and very distinctly are all true. But that left the single difficulty of properly noticing which things are the ones we conceive distinctly.[1]

After that, I reflected on the fact that I had doubts and that, as a result, my being was not completely perfect, for I saw clearly that it was a greater perfection to know than to doubt. I realized that I should seek out where I had learned to think of something more perfect than I was. And I concluded that obviously this must be something with a nature which was, in effect, more perfect. As for the thoughts which I had of several other things outside of me, like the sky, the earth, light, heat, and a thousand others, I was not worried about knowing where they came from, because I did not notice anything in them which seemed to me to make them superior to myself. Thus, I was able to think that, if they were true, that was because of their dependence on my nature, in so far as it had some perfection and, if they were not true, I held them from nothing, that is to say, that they were in me because I had some defect. But that could not be the same with the idea of a being more perfect than mine. For to hold that idea from nothing would be manifestly impossible. And because it is no less unacceptable that something more perfect should be a consequence of and dependent on something less perfect than that something should come from nothing, I could not derive this idea from myself. Thus, I concluded that the idea had been put in me by a nature which was truly more

[1]The translation of the crucial and much-discussed words *clairement* and *distinctement* as *clearly* and *distinctly* is extremely common. Descartes' *Principia Philosophiae*, 1:45-6, discusses (in Latin) his use of these terms: "I call an idea clear (*claram*) when it is present and manifest to a mind focusing on it, just as we say we perceive something clearly when it is present to the observing eye, and stimulates it sufficiently strongly and fully. I call an idea distinct (*distinctam*) which, while it is clear, is separated and marked off from everything else in such a way that it consists of absolutely nothing which is not clear." Descartes apparently has in mind the clarity and distinctiveness of mathematical propositions. Truth thus comes, not from sense perception or imagination but from rational intuition.

perfect than I was, even one which contained in itself all the perfections about which I could have some idea, that is to say, to explain myself in a single phrase, a nature which was God. To this I added the fact that, since I know about some perfections which I do not have, I was not the only being which existed (here I will freely use, if you will permit me, the language of the schools), but it must of necessity be the case that there was some other more perfect being, on whom I depended and from whom I had acquired all that I had. For if I had been alone and independent of everything else, so that I derived from myself all perfection, no matter how small, of the perfect being, I would have been able to have from myself, for the same reason, all the additional perfections which I knew I lacked, and thus be myself infinite, eternal, immutable, all knowing, all powerful, and finally have all the perfections which I could observe as present in God. For, following the reasoning which I have just made, to know the nature of God, to the extent that my reasoning is able to do that, I only had to think about of all the things of which I found some idea within me and consider whether it was a sign of perfection to possess them or not. And I was confident that none of those ideas which indicated some imperfection were in God, but that all the others were there, since I perceived that doubt, inconstancy, sadness, and similar things could not be in God, in view of the fact that I myself would have been very pleased to be free of them. Then, in addition, I had ideas about several sensible and corporeal things. For although I supposed that I was asleep and that everything which I saw or imagined was false, nonetheless I could not deny that the ideas had truly been in my thoughts. But because I had already recognized in myself very clearly that intelligent nature is distinct from corporeal nature, when I considered that all composite natures indicate dependency and that dependency is manifestly a defect, I judged from this that God's perfection could not consist of being composed of these two natures, and that thus He was not, but that if there were some bodies in the world or even some intelligences or other natures which were not completely perfect, their being had to depend on God's power, in such a way as they could not subsist for a single moment without Him.

After that I wanted to look for other truths, and I proposed to myself the subject matter of geometricians, which I understood as a continuous body or a space extended indefinitely in length, width, and height or depth, divisible into various parts, which could have various figures and sizes and be moved or transposed in all sorts of ways, for the geometricians assume all that in their subject matter. I glanced through some of their simplest proofs, and having observed that this grand certainty which all the world attributes to them is founded only on the fact that they plan these proofs clearly, following the rule which I have so often stated, I notice also that there is nothing at all in their proofs which assures me of the existence of their objects. So, for example, I do see that, if we assume a triangle, it must be the case that its three angles are equal to two right angles, but, in spite of that, I do not see anything which assures me that there is a triangle in the world. But, by contrast, once I returned to an examination of the idea which I had of a perfect being, I found that that being contains the idea of existence in the same way as the fact the three angles of a triangle are equal to two right angles is contained in the idea of a triangle, or that in a sphere all the parts are equidistant from the centre, or it is even more evident, and that, as a result, it is as just as certain that God, this perfect being, is or exists as any geometric proof can be.

But the reason there are several people who persuade themselves that there are difficulties in understanding this and even knowing what their soul is, as well, is that they never raise their minds above matters of sense experience and that they are so accustomed not to consider anything except by imagining it, which is a way of thinking in particular of material things, so that everything which is not imaginable seems to them unintelligible. This point is obvious enough in the fact that even the philosophers in the schools maintain the axiom that there is nothing in the understanding which has not first of all been in the senses. But it is certain that the ideas of God and the soul have never been present in sense experience. It seemed to me that those who want to use their imagination to understand these things are acting just as if they want to use their eyes to hear sounds or smell odours, except that there is still this difference, that the sense of sight provides us no less assurance of the truth of what it sees than do the sense of smell or hearing; whereas, neither our imagination nor our senses can assure us of anything unless our understanding intercedes.

Finally, if there are still some people who are insufficiently persuaded of the existence of God and their soul by the reasons I have provided, I would like them to know that everything else which they perhaps are more confident about in their thinking, like having a body and knowing that there are stars and an earth, and things like that, are less certain than God's existence. For although one has a moral assurance about these things, which makes doubting them appear at least extravagant, nonetheless, unless one is an unreasonable being, when a question of metaphysical certainty is involved, one cannot deny that there is insufficient material here to make one completely confident, for we notice that one can imagine in the same way while sleeping that one has another body and that one sees other stars and another earth, without such things existing. For what is the source of our knowledge that the thoughts which come while dreaming are false, rather than the others, seeing that often they are no less lively and distinct? And if the best minds study this matter as much as they please, I do not think that they will be able to give any reason which will be sufficient to remove this doubt unless they presuppose the existence of God. First of all, the very principle which I have so often taken as a rule—only to recognize as true all those things which we conceive very clearly and very distinctly—is guaranteed only because of the fact that God is or exists, that He is a perfect being, and that everything which is in us comes from Him. From that it follows that our ideas or notions, being real things which come from God, to the extent that they are clear and distinct, in that respect cannot be anything but true. Consequently, if we often enough have some ideas or notions which contain something false, that can only be those which contain some confusion and obscurity, because in this they participate in nothing, that is to say, they are so confused in us only because we are not completely perfect. And it is evident that it is no less repugnant that falsity or imperfection, in itself, should come from God than that truth or perfection should come from nothingness. But if we did not know that everything real and true within us comes from a perfect and infinite being, then no matter how clear and distinct our ideas were, we would not have a single reason to assure us that they had the perfection of being true.

Now, after the knowledge of God and the soul in this way has made us certain of this rule, it is really easy to see that the dreams which we imagine while asleep should not, in any way, make us doubt the truth of the thoughts we have while awake. For if it happened, even while we were sleeping, that we had some really distinct idea, as, for example, in the case of a geometer inventing some new proof, the fact that he is asleep does not prevent it from being true, and as for error, it doesn't matter that the most common dreams we have, which consist of representing to us various objects in the same way as our external senses do, can give us occasion to challenge the truth of such ideas, because these ideas can also mislead us often enough without our being asleep, as, for example, when those people suffering from jaundice see all objects as yellow, or when the stars or other bodies at a great distant appear to us much smaller than they are. For, finally, whether we are awake or asleep, we should never allow ourselves to be persuaded except by the evidence of our reason. And people should note that I say of our reason and not of our imagination or of our senses, since even though we see the sun very clearly, we should not for that reason judge that it is only the size which we see it, and we can easily imagine distinctly the head of a lion mounted on the body of goat, without having to conclude, because of that, there is a chimera in the world.[1] For reason does not dictate to us that what we see or imagine in this way is true, but it does dictate to us that all our ideas or notions must have some foundation in truth, for it would not be possible that God, who is com-

---

[1] A chimera is a mythological Greek monster, made up of different animals.

pletely perfect and totally truthful, put them in us without that. Because our reasoning is never so evident or complete during sleeping as while we are awake, although then sometimes our imaginations are as vital or explicit, or more so, reason also dictates to us that our ideas cannot all be true, because we are not completely perfect—those which contain the truth must without exception come in those we experience while awake rather than in those we have while asleep.

PART FIVE

I would be very pleased to continue and make you see here all the chain of other truths which I deduced from these first ones. But because that would require that I talked of several questions which are controversial among scholars, things I do not want to get mixed up with, I think it would be better to refrain from that and speak only in general about what these matters are, so that I leave it to wiser heads to judge if it would be useful for the public to be informed about more particular details. I have always lived firm in the resolution that I had taken not to assume any other principle than the one which I have just used to demonstrate the existence of God and the soul, and to accept nothing as true which did not seem to me more clear and more certain than the proofs of geometers had seemed to me previously. Nonetheless, I venture to say that, not only did I find a way of satisfying myself in a short time concerning all the difficult principles which people are accustomed to deal with in philosophy, but also I noticed certain laws which God has established in nature in such a way and of which he has impressed such notions in our souls, that after we have reflected on them sufficiently, we cannot doubt that they are precisely observed in everything which exists or which acts in the world. Then, as I considered the consequence of these laws, it seemed to me that I had discovered several truths more useful and more important than everything which I had previously learned or even hoped to learn.

But since I attempted to explain the principles in a treatise which certain considerations prevented me from publishing, I do not know how better to make them known than stating here in summary form what that treatise contains. Before writing that text, I had the intention of including in it all that I thought I knew concerning the nature of material things. But just as painters cannot portray equally well in a flat picture all the various surfaces of a solid body and choose one of the main surfaces, which they set by itself facing the light and, by placing the others in shadows, do not allow anything to appear more than one can see by looking at them, in the same way, fearing that I could not put in my discourse everything I had in my thoughts, I tried only to reveal there fairly fully what I understood about light, and then at the appropriate time, to add something about the sun and the fixed stars, because almost all light comes from them, about the heavens, because they transmit light; about the planets, comets, and the earth, because they reflect light, and in particular about all the bodies on earth, because they are coloured, or transparent, or luminous, and finally about man, because he is the one who looks at these things. Even so, in order to shade in all these things a little and to be able to speak more freely of what I was judging, without being obliged to follow or to refute received opinions among the scholars, I resolved to leave everyone here to their disputes and to speak only of what would happen in a new world, if God now created somewhere in imaginary space enough material to compose it, and if He set in motion, in a varied and disorderly way, the various parts of this material, so that it created a chaos as confused as poets could make it, and then afterwards He did nothing other than lend His ordinary help to nature and allow it to act according to the laws which He established.[1] So first of all I described this material and tried to picture it in such a way that there is nothing in the world, it seems to me, clearer and more intelligible, except what has been said from time to time about God and the soul. For I even explicitly assumed that in the world there were none of those forms or qualities which people argue about in the schools, nor, in general, anything the knowledge of which was not so natural to our souls that we could not even pretend to remain ignorant of it. In addition, I made known the laws of nature, and without basing my reasoning on any principle other than the infinite perfections of God, I tried to demonstrate all of these laws about which one could entertain any doubts, to show that they are such that, although God could have created several worlds, there would not be one where these failed to be observed. After that, I showed how the greatest part of material in chaos would have to, as a result of these laws, organize and arrange itself in a certain way which made it similar to our heavens, how, in so doing, some of its parts must have made up an earth and some parts planets and comets, and some other parts a sun and fixed stars. And at this point, dwelling on the subject of light, I explained at some length the nature of light which must be found in the sun and the stars, how from there it crossed in an instant the immense distances of heavenly space, and how it is reflected from the planets and comets towards the earth. To this I added several things concerning the material, the arrangement, the movements, and all the various qualities of these heavens and these stars. Consequently, I thought I had said enough about these matters to make known the fact that one observes nothing in

---

[1]Descartes is here describing a thought experiment in which he imagines how the world might have developed historically from material distributed randomly in the universe and then acting in accordance with certain natural laws. The idea is potentially dangerous because it goes against the description of creation given in Genesis. Hence, later on Descartes explicitly denies that he is claiming the process he is summarizing actually took place.

these features of this world which must not, or at least could not, appear entirely similar to those of the world which I described. From there I went on to speak in particular about the earth, about how, although I had expressly assumed that God had placed no heaviness in the material of which it is composed, all its parts could not help tending precisely to its centre, how, having water and air on its surface, the arrangement of the heavens and the stars, and particularly of the moon, had to create on earth an ebb and flow similar in all its features to the ones we see in our oceans, and, beyond that, a certain flow in the water as well as in the air, from east to west, like the one we also observe between the tropics, how the mountains, seas, fountains, and rivers can naturally form out of that, how earth's metals come into the mines, and how the plants on earth grow in the fields, and, in general, how all the things we call mixed or composite could be produced on earth. And, among other things, because I know of nothing, other than the stars, which produces light except fire, I studied to understand really clearly everything associated with the nature of fire, how it arises, how it is nourished, how sometimes it has heat without light and sometimes light without heat, how it can introduce various colours in different bodies, as well as various other qualities, how it melts some things and makes others harder, how it can consume almost everything or convert it into ash and smoke, and finally how, out of these cinders, simply by the violence of its actions, it makes glass. For this transformation of cinders into glass seemed to be as wonderful as anything else which happens in nature, and I took particular pleasure in describing it.

However, I did not want to conclude from all these things that this world was created in the fashion which I was proposing. For it is much more probable that God made the world from the beginning just what it had to be. But it is certain, and this is an opinion commonly accepted among theologians, that the actions by which God now preserves the world are exactly the same as the method by which He created it, in such a way that even if He did not give it at the start any form other than a chaos, providing that He had first established the laws of nature and had given His assistance, so that it would act as it usually does, we can believe, without denying the miracle of creation, that because of these facts alone all purely material things would have been able, over time, to become the way we now observe them, and their nature is much easier to conceive when one sees them born gradually in this way than if one thinks of them only as made all at once in a finished state.[1]

---

[1]Here Descartes is again coming close to potentially dangerous speculations. To propose that God's actions in developing the world are subject to natural laws, even if God is the origin of those laws, is to suggest that there are some restrictions on God's later actions (i.e., His inter-

[Footnote continues]

From the description of the inanimate bodies and of plants, I moved onto the bodies of animals and especially the body of man. But because I did not yet have sufficient knowledge to speak of that in the same way as of other things, that is to say, to speak of effects in terms of causes, by revealing the seeds and the methods by which nature had to produce them, I contented myself with assuming that God formed the human body completely like one of our own, both in the external shape of its limbs and in the arrangement of its inner organs, without making them of any material other than the one which I had described and without, at the start, placing in that body any reasonable soul or any other thing to serve the body as a vegetative or sensitive soul, except that He kindled in its heart one of those fires without light which I had already explained and which I conceived as in no way different in its nature from the fire which heats hay when it is stored before it is dry or which makes new wines bubble when they are allowed to ferment on the crushed grapes. For, by examining the functions which, as a result of this assumption, could be present in this body, I found precisely all those which could be in us without our being able to think, and thus those functions to which our soul, that is to say, that distinct part of the body whose nature is solely to think (as I have said above) does not contribute, functions which are exactly the same as those in which we can say the animals without reason are similar to us. But in doing this, I could not find any of those which, because they are dependent on thought, are the only ones which pertain to us, to the extent that we are men; whereas, I found all of them afterwards, once I assumed the God had created a reasonable soul and joined it to this body in the particular way which I described.

But so that you can see how I dealt with this material in that treatise, I want to put in here the explanation for the movement of the heart and the arteries, the first and the most universal thing which one observes in animals. From that one will easily assess what one should think of all the others. And so that people have less difficulty understanding what I am going to say, I would like those who are not versed in anatomy to take the trouble, before reading this, to have the heart of some large animal with lungs dissected in front of them. For it is in all respects sufficiently similar to the heart in man. And I would like them to have demonstrated to them

ventions and actions in the world must conform to those laws). However, the value of thinking about the development of the world as a historical process guided by laws (rather than as the product of the divine miracle of Creation) is that it enables human beings to come to a rational understanding of nature as a process with material causes and effects and thus makes the modern scientific study of nature possible, even if only in a thought experiment. There is no reason to assume that Descartes is not being perfectly sincere here, although later writers did use the same argument about a hypothetical thought experiment simply as a rhetorical device (e.g., Rousseau in the *Second Discourse*).

the two chambers or cavities which are in that heart. First, there is one chamber on its right side, to which two very large tubes correspond, that is, the *vena cava*, which is the principal receptacle of blood and, as it were, the trunk of the tree of which all the other veins of the body are the branches, and the *vena arteriosa*, which has, with that label, been poorly named, because it is, in fact, an artery, the one which, originating at the heart, divides up, after leaving the heart, into several branches, which go out to distribute themselves throughout the lungs.[1] Then there is the chamber on the left side of the heart, to which, in the same way, two tubes correspond, which are as large or larger than the ones just mentioned: that is, the venous artery, which is also misnamed, because it is nothing but a vein which comes from the lungs, where it is divided into several branches interwoven with those from the arterial vein and with those associated with the tube called the windpipe, through which air enters for respiration; and the large artery which, leaving the heart, sends its branches throughout the body. I would also like someone to point out carefully to them the eleven small strips of skin which, just like so many small doors, open and close the four openings in these two chambers, that is, three at the entry of the *vena cava*, where they are so arranged that they cannot in any way prevent the blood contained in the *vena cava* from flowing into the right chamber of the heart and, at the same time, effectively prevent its ability to flow out; three gates at the entry of arterial vein, which, being arranged in precisely the opposite way, easily allow the blood in this chamber to move toward the lungs but do not allow the blood in the lungs to return to that chamber of the heart. Then, in the same way, there are two other strips of membrane at the opening to the venous artery which allow the blood from the lungs to flow towards the left chamber of the heart, but prevent its return, and there are three at the entry of the great artery which allow blood to leave the heart but prevent it from returning there. There is no need to seek for any reason for the number of these membranes, beyond the fact that since the opening of the venous artery is an oval, because of its location, it can be readily closed with two; whereas, since the others are round, they can be more easily closed with three. In addition, I would like people to notice that the large artery and the arterial vein have a composition much harder and firmer than the venous artery and the *vena cava*, that these last two get bigger before entering the heart and there make a structure similar to two small sacks, called the auricles of the heart, which are composed of flesh like that of the heart, that there is always more heat in the heart than in any other place in the body; and finally that, if any drop of blood enters its cavities, this heat in the heart is capable of making the drop quickly swell and expand, just as all liquors

[1]*vena arteriosa*: arterial vein, now called the pulmonary artery.

generally do when one lets them fall drop by drop into some really hot container.

After all that, I have no need to say anything else to explain the movement of the heart, other than the following: when its cavities are not full of blood, then necessarily blood flows from the *vena cava* into the right chamber and from the venous artery into the left, because these two blood vessels are always full and their openings, which are oriented towards the heart, cannot then be blocked. But as soon as two drops of blood have entered the heart in this way, one in each of its chambers, these drops, which could only be of a considerable size because the openings through which they enter are very large and the vessels they come from are really full of blood, become thinner and expand, on account of the heat they encounter there, as a result of which they make the entire heart expand, and then they push against and close the five small gates which stand at the openings of the two vessels from which these drops of blood have come, thus preventing any more blood from moving down into the heart. And, continuing to become increasingly thinner, the drops of blood push against and open the six other small gates which stand at the opening of the two other vessels, through which they flow out, in this way causing all the branches of the arterial vein and great artery to expand, almost at the same instant as the heart, which immediately afterwards contracts, as do these arteries as well, because the blood which has entered them gets colder again there, and their six small gates close once more. Then the five valves on the *vena cava* and the venous artery re-open, and allow passage of two more drops of blood, which, once more, make the heart and the arteries expand, just as in the preceding steps. And because the blood which enters the heart in this manner passes through these two small sacks called auricles, this motion causes the movement of the auricles to be the opposite of the heart's movement—they contract when the heart expands. As for the rest, so that those who do not understand the force of mathematical proofs and who are not accustomed to distinguishing true reasons from probable reasons do not venture to deny this matter without examining it, I wish to advise them that this movement which I have just explained is as necessarily a result of the mere arrangement of the organs which one can see in the heart with one's own eyes and of the heat which one can feel there with one's fingers and of the nature of blood which one can recognize from experience, as the movement of a clock is necessarily a result of the force, the placement, and the shape of its counter-weights and wheels.[1]

---

[1] The point of this long example, taken directly from the work of the English doctor William Harvey, who published his pioneering book on the heart and circulation of the blood in 1628,

[Footnote continues]

But if someone asks how the blood in the veins does not exhaust itself as it flows continually into the heart in this way and how the arteries are not overfilled because all the blood which passes through the heart goes into them, there is no need for me to say anything in reply other than what has already been written by an English doctor, to whom we must give the honour of having broken the ice in this area and of being the first to teach that there are several small passages at the extremities of the arteries through which the blood which they receive from the heart enters into the small branches of the veins, from where it proceeds to move once again towards the heart, so that its passage is nothing other than a constant circulation. He proves this really well by the common experience of surgeons who, having bound up an arm moderately tightly above a place where they have opened a vein, cause the blood to flow out more abundantly than if they had not tied the arm. And the opposite happens if they place the binding below the cut, between the hand and the opening, or if they make the binding above the opening very tight. For it is clear that the binding, when moderately tight, can only prevent the blood which is already in the arm from returning towards the heart by the veins, but in doing that the binding does not stop the blood from continuing to flow to the place from the arteries, because the arteries are situated below the veins and because the skin of the arteries, being harder, is less easy to press down. Thus, the blood which comes from the heart tends to move with more force through the arteries towards the hand than it does in returning from the hand towards the heart through the veins. And because this blood leaves the arm by the opening in one of the veins, it must necessarily be the case that there are some passages below this binding, that is to say, towards the extremities of the arm, through which it can come there from the arteries. He [Harvey] also demonstrates really well what he says about the flow of blood through certain small membranes which are so arranged in various places along the veins that they do not allow blood to move in the veins from the middle of the body towards the extremities, but only to return from the extremities towards the heart. Moreover, he demonstrates this by an experiment which shows that all the blood which is in the body can leave it in a very little time by a single artery, if it is cut, even if it has been tightly bound really close to the heart and cut between the heart and the binding, so that one simply could not imagine any explanation other than that the blood flowing out is coming from the heart.

But there are several other things which attest to the fact that the true cause of this movement of blood is as I have described it. For, firstly, the

is to illustrate and stress the mechanical and clock-like regularity of physical nature, especially the human body.

difference which one notices between the blood which comes from the veins and the blood which flows out of the arteries could come about only if the blood is rarefied and, as it were, distilled in passing through the heart. It is more subtle, more lively, and warmer immediately after leaving the heart, that is to say, in the arteries, than it is shortly before entering the heart, that is to say, when it is in the veins. And if one pays attention, one will find that this difference is only readily apparent close to the heart and not so evident in places which are more distant from it. Then, the hardness of the skins making up the arterial vein and the large artery shows sufficiently well that the blood beats against them with greater force than it does against the veins. And why would the left chamber of the heart and the great artery be more ample and larger than the right chamber and the arterial vein, if it were not for the fact that the blood of the venous artery, which has only been in the lungs since passing through the heart, is more subtle and more strongly and more easily rarefied than the blood which comes immediately from the *vena cava*? And what could doctors diagnose by testing the pulse, if they did not know, in keeping with the fact that blood changes its nature, that it can be rarefied by the heat of the heart more or less strongly and more or less quickly than before? And if one examines how this heat is transferred to the other limbs, is it not necessary to admit that it is by means of the blood, which, passing through the heart, is re-heated in it and from there spreads throughout the entire body? That is the reason why, if one takes blood from some part of the body, in that very process one takes the heat, and even if the heart were as hot as a burning fire, it would not be sufficient to re-heat the feet and the hands as much as it does, if it did not continually send new blood there. From this we also understand that the true purpose of respiration is to bring sufficient fresh air into the lungs to ensure that the blood which comes from the right chamber of the heart, where it has been rarefied and, as it were, changed into vapour, thickens and changes back again into blood, before falling back into the left chamber, without which it would not be fit to serve as nourishment for the fire there. What confirms this is that we observe that the animals which have no lungs also have only one cavity in the heart and that children, who cannot use their lungs while they are closed up in their mother's womb, have an opening through which blood flows from the *vena cava* into the left cavity of the heart and a passage by which the blood comes from the arterial vein into the large artery without passing through the lungs. Next, how would digestion take place in the stomach, if the heart did not send heat there through the arteries and with that some of the more easily flowing parts of the blood which help to dissolve the food which has been sent there? And the action which converts the juice of this food into blood—surely that is easy to understand, if one considers that it is distilled, as it passes and re-passes through the heart, perhaps more than one or two hundred times each day? What else do we need to explain nutrition and the production of the various humours in the body, other than to say that the force with which the blood, as it gets rarefied, passes from the heart towards the extremities of the arteries, brings it about that some portions of it stop among those parts of the limbs where they are, and there take the place of some other parts which the blood pushes away, and that, depending on the situation or the shape or the smallness of the pores which these parts of blood encounter, some of them go off to certain places rather than to others, in the same way that anyone can see with various screens, which, being pierced in different ways, serve to separate various grains from one another? Finally, what is most remarkable in all this is the generation of animal spirits which resemble a very slight wind or rather a very pure and very lively flame which, by climbing continually in great quantities from the heart into the brain, goes from there through the nerves into the muscles and gives movement to all the limbs, without it being necessary to imagine any other cause which has the effect of making the most agitated and most penetrating parts of blood, those most appropriate for making up these animal spirits, move towards the brain rather than elsewhere, other than that the arteries which carry these parts of the blood are those which come from the heart toward the brain by the most direct route and that, following the laws of mechanics, which are the same as nature's laws, when several things collectively tend to move towards the same place where there is insufficient room for all of them, as the parts of blood which leave the left cavity of the heart tend towards the brain, the most feeble and less agitated parts must be turned away from the brain by the strongest parts. In this way, only the latter parts reach the brain.

I explained in particular detail all these things in the treatise which I had planned to publish previously. And then I demonstrated what the nerves and muscles in the human body must be made of, so that the animal spirits, once inside the nerves, would have the power to move its limbs, as one sees that heads, for a little while after being cut off, continue to move and bite the earth, in spite of the fact that they are no longer animated. I also showed what changes must take places in the brain to cause the waking state, sleep, and dreams, how light, sounds, smells, tastes, heat, and all the other qualities of external objects could imprint various ideas on the brain through the mediation of the senses, just as hunger, thirst, and the other inner passions can also send their ideas to the brain; what must be understood by common sense where these ideas are taken in, by memory which preserves them, and by fantasy which can change them in various ways and compose new ones, and, in the same way, distribute animal spirits to the muscles and make the limbs of the body move in all the different ways—in relation to the objects which present themselves to the senses and in relation to the interior physical passions—just as our bodies can move themselves without being led by the will. None of this will seem strange to those who know how many varieties of *automata*, or moving machines, human industry can make, by using only very few pieces in comparison with the huge number of bones, muscles, nerves, arteries, veins, and all the other parts in the body of each animal. They will look on this body as a machine, which, having been made by the hand of God, is incomparably better ordered and more inherently admirable in its movements than any of those which human beings could have invented. And here, in particular, I stopped to reveal that if there were machines which had the organs and the external shape of a monkey or of some other animal without reason, we would have no way of recognizing that they were not exactly the same nature as the animals; whereas, if there was a machine shaped like our bodies which imitated our actions as much as is morally possible, we would always have two very certain ways of recognizing that they were not, for all their resemblance, true human beings. The first of these is that they would never be able to use words or other signs to make words as we do to declare our thoughts to others. For one can easily imagine a machine made in such a way that it expresses words, even that it expresses some words relevant to some physical actions which bring about some change in its organs (for example, if one touches it in some spot, the machine asks what it is that one wants to say to it; if in another spot, it cries that one has hurt it, and things like that), but one cannot imagine a machine that arranges words in various ways to reply to the sense of everything said in its presence, as the most stupid human beings are capable of doing. The second test is that, although these machines might do several things as well or perhaps better than we do, they are inevitably lacking in some others, through which we would discover that they act, not by knowledge, but only by the arrangement of their organs. For, whereas reason is a universal instrument which can serve in all sorts of encounters, these organs need some particular arrangement for each particular action. As a result of that, it is morally impossible that there is in a machine's organs sufficient variety to act in all the events of life in the same way that our reason empowers us to act. Now, by these two same means, one can also recognize the difference between human beings and beasts. For it is really remarkable that there are no men so dull and stupid, including even idiots, who are not capable of putting together different words and of creating out of them a conversation through which they make their thoughts known; by contrast, there is no other animal, no matter how perfect and how successful it might be, which can do anything like that. And this inability does not come about from a lack of organs For we see that magpies and parrots can emit words, as we can, but nonetheless cannot talk the way we can, that is to say, giving evidence that they are thinking about what they are uttering; whereas, men who are born deaf and dumb are deprived of organs which other people use to speak—just as much as or more than the animals—but they have a habit of inventing on their own some signs by which they can make themselves understood to those who, being usually with them, have the spare time to learn their language. And this point attests not merely to the fact that animals have less reason than men, but to the fact that they have none at all. For we see that it takes very little for someone to learn how to speak, and since we observe inequality among the animals of the same species just as much as among human beings, and see that some are easier to train than others, it would be incredible that a monkey or a parrot which was the most perfect of his species was not equivalent in speaking to the most stupid child or at least a child with a troubled brain, unless their soul had a nature totally different from our own. And one should not confuse words with natural movements which attest to the passions and can be imitated by machines as well as by animals, nor should one think, like some ancients, that animals talk, although we do not understand their language. For if that were true, because they have several organs related to our own, they could just as easily make themselves understood to us as to the animals like them. Another truly remarkable thing is that, although there are several animals which display more industry in some of their actions than we do, we nonetheless see that they do not display that at all in many other actions. Thus, the fact that they do better than we do does not prove that they have a mind, for, if that were the case, they would have more of it than any of us and would do better in all other things; it rather shows that they have no reason at all, and that it is nature which has activated them according to the arrangement of their organs—just as one sees that a clock, which is composed only of wheels and springs, can keep track of the hours and measure time more accurately than we can, for all our care.[1]

After that, I described the reasonable soul and revealed that it cannot be inferred in any way from the power of matter, like the other things I have spoken about, but that it must be expressly created, and I described how it is not sufficient that it is lodged in the human body like a pilot in his ship, except perhaps to move its limbs, but that it is necessary that the soul is joined and united more closely with the body, so that it has, in addition, feelings and appetites similar to ours and thus makes up a true human being.[2] As for the rest, here I went on at some length on the subject of the soul, because it is among the most important. For, apart from the error of

---

[1] For Descartes, then, animals are merely machines, and the sounds they emit are essentially the same as the sounds made by machines.

[2] Descartes here announces one of the most challenging issues arising from his views. If the body is mechanical and the soul is not and if they must interact in some way, then how and where does that interaction takes place? How can one explain consciousness in mechanistic terms? This is still the thorniest problem in modern biology.

those who deny God, which I believe I have adequately refuted above, there is nothing which distances feeble minds from the right road of virtue more readily than to imagine that the soul of animals is the same nature as our own and that thus we have nothing either to fear or to hope for after this life, any more than flies and ants do; whereas, once one knows how different they are, one understands much better the reasons which prove that the nature of our souls is totally independent of the body, and thus it is not at all subject to dying along with the body. Then, to the extent that one cannot see other causes which destroy the soul, one is naturally led to judge from that that the soul is immortal.

PART SIX

It is now three years since I reached the end of the treatise which contains all these things and since I started to revise it in order to put it into the hands of a printer. Then I learned that people to whom I defer and whose authority over my actions could hardly be less than my own reason over my thoughts had expressed disapproval of an opinion about physics published a little earlier by someone else.[1] I do not wish to say that I subscribed to that opinion, but, although I had observed in it nothing before their censure which I could imagine prejudicial to religion or the state, and thus nothing which would have prevented me from writing it if reason had persuaded me, this made me afraid that there might nonetheless be something among my opinions where I had gone astray, notwithstanding the great care I always took not to accept new ideas into my beliefs for which I did not have very certain proofs and not to write anything which would work to anyone's disadvantage. This was sufficient to oblige me to alter my resolution to publish my opinions. For although the reasons I had adopted earlier had been very strong, my inclination, which has always led me to hate the profession of producing books, made me immediately find enough other reasons to excuse myself in this matter. And, given the nature of these reasons, on one side or the other, not only am I quite interested in stating them here, but the public may perhaps also be interested in knowing them.

I have never made a great deal of the things which come from my own mind, so while I gathered no other fruits from the method I was using, other than that I satisfied myself concerning some difficulties in the speculative sciences or else that I tried to regulate my morals by reasons which my method taught me, I did not think myself obliged to write any-

---

[1] The phrase "someone else" is a reference to Galileo, whose publication in defence of Copernicus' sun-centered model of the solar system (in 1632) got him into serious difficulties with the church.

thing. For where morals are concerned, every person is so full of his own good sense that it would be possible to find as many reformers as heads, if it was permitted to people other than those God has established as sovereigns over his people or those to whom he has given sufficient grace and zeal to be prophets to try changing anything in our morality. Although my speculations pleased me a great deal, I thought that other people also had their own speculations which pleased them perhaps even more. But immediately after I had acquired some general notions concerning physics and, by starting to test them on various particular difficulties, had noticed just where they could lead and how much they differed from principles which people have used up to the present time, I thought that I could not keep them hidden without sinning greatly against the law which obliges us to promote as much as we can the general good of all men. For my notions had made me see that it is possible to reach understandings which are extremely useful for life and that instead of the speculative philosophy which is taught in the schools, we can find a practical philosophy by which, through understanding the force and actions of fire, water, air, stars, heavens, and all the other bodies which surround us as distinctly as we understand the various crafts of our artisans, we could use them in the same way for all applications for which they are appropriate and thus make ourselves, as it were, the masters and possessors of nature.[1] But it was not only a desire for to invent an infinite number of devices which might enable us to enjoy without effort the fruits of the earth and all the commodities found in it, but mainly also my desire for the preservation of our health, which is, without doubt, the principal benefit and the foundation of all the other benefits in this life. For even the mind depends so much on the temperament and the condition of the organs of the body that, if it is possible to find some means to make human beings generally wiser and more skilful than they have been up to this point, I believe we must seek that in medicine. It is true that the medicine now practiced contains few things which are remarkably useful. But without having any design to denigrate it, I am confident that there is no one, not even those who make a living from medicine, who would not claim that everything we know in medicine is almost nothing in comparison to what remains to be known about it and that we could liberate ourselves from an infinity of illnesses, both of the body and the mind, and also perhaps even of the infirmities of ageing, if we had sufficient knowledge of their causes and of all the remedies which nature has provided for us. Now, intending to spend all my life in research into such a necessary science and having encountered a road which seemed to me such that one should infallibly find this

---

[1] In this famous statement Descartes makes clear one of the major purposes of the new natural philosophy (science): to gain power over nature.

science by following it, unless one was prevented either by the brevity of one's life or by the lack of experiments, I judged that there was no better remedy against these two obstacles than to communicate faithfully to the public the little I had found and to invite good minds to try to move on further, by contributing, each according to his own inclination and power, to the experiments which need to be conducted and also by communicating to the public everything they learn, so that the most recent people begin where the previous ones have finished. If we thus joined the lives and labours of many people, collectively we might go much further than each particular person could.

Besides, I noticed that, where experiments are concerned, they are increasingly necessary as one's knowledge advances, for at the beginning it is better to conduct only those which present themselves to our sense and which we cannot ignore, provided that we engage in a little reflection, rather than to seek out more rare and recondite experiments, because these rarer ones are often misleading, when we do not yet know the causes of the more common phenomena, and the circumstances on which they depend are almost always so particular and so precise, that it is very difficult to observe them. But in this work I kept to the following order: first, I tried to find the general principles or the first causes of everything which exists or could exist in the world, without considering anything germane to my purpose other than the fact that God alone created the world, not deducing anything additional, other than certain grains of truth which are naturally in our souls. After that, I examined what were the first and most common effects we could deduce from these causes. By doing that, it seems to me, I found the heavens, the stars, and earth, and even on the earth water, air, fire, minerals, and some other things, the sort which are the most common of all and the simplest, and thus the easiest to know. Then, when I wanted to move down to more particular matters, so many varied ones presented themselves to me that I did not think it would be possible for the human mind to distinguish the forms or species of bodies on the earth from an infinity of others which could exist there if the will of God had put them there and, thus, that one could not adapt them to our use, unless one proceeded to the causes through the effects and made use of several particular experiments. After that, I turned my mind onto all the objects which had ever presented themselves to my senses. I venture to say that I did not notice in them anything which I could not explain easily enough by the principles which I had found. But I must also confess that the power of nature is so ample and vast and its principles are so simple and so general that I observed hardly any particular effect which I did not immediately understand as being capable of being deduced in several different ways, so that my greatest difficulty is usually to find on which of these ways the effect depends. In dealing with this matter, I did not know any expedient other than, once again, to look for some experiments which would be such that their outcomes would not be the same if one of these ways had to explain it rather than some other way. As for the rest, I am now at a point where I perceive well enough, it seems to me, the method one has to use to make most of those experiments which can serve for this purpose. But I also see that they are of such a kind and that there are so many of them that neither my hands nor my income, even if I it was a thousand times more than it is, could suffice for all of them, so that from now on my progress in understanding nature will be proportional to the means I have for conducting more or fewer experiments. This was what I promised myself I would make known in the treatise which I had written, as well as showing in it the practical value which the public could gain from these experiments so clearly that I would oblige all those who wished to promote the general well being of man, that is to say, all those who are truly virtuous and who are not false by pretending to virtue or merely virtuous by public opinion, to communicate to me all the experiments which they have already made, as well as to help me in researching those which remain to be done.

But since that time I have had other reasons which made me change my mind and think that I really must continue to write down all matters which I judged to have some importance, to the extent that I discovered truth in them, and to bring to my writing the same care that I would if I wanted it published, so that I would have more time to examine such things well, since there is no doubt that one always looks more closely at what one thinks many people must see than at what one does only for oneself, and often matters which seemed to me true when I began to think of them appeared false to me when I wished to put them on paper. By writing things down, I would not lose any opportunity to benefit the public, if I could, and, if my writings are worth anything, those who have them after my death could use them wherever they were most relevant. But I thought I must not, on any account, agree that they be published during my life, so as to prevent the hostility and controversies which they could perhaps arouse and the sort of reputation which I could acquire from giving me any occasion to waste the time which I planned to use to instruct myself. For although it is true that each man is obliged to provide as much as is in him for the good of others and that there is no value whatsoever in anything which has no benefit for anyone, nevertheless it is also true that we should care about things more distant than the present and that it is good to forget about things which might bring some benefit to those now living when one's intention is to create other things which will bring more benefits to our descendants. In fact, I really wanted people to understand that the little I had learned up to this point is almost nothing in comparison with what I am ignorant of and what I do not despair of being able to learn. For it is almost the same with those who discover truth little by little in the sciences as it is with those who, once they start to become rich, have less trouble in making large acquisitions than they did previously, when they were poorer, in making much smaller ones. Or, again, one can compare them to leaders of armies whose forces usually grow in proportion to their victories and who, in order to capture towns and provinces, need more leadership to maintain their forces after the loss of a battle than they do after winning one. For it is truly a matter of giving battle when one tries to overcome all the difficulties and mistakes which prevent us from reaching an understanding of the truth. And it is a battle loss when one accepts some false opinion concerning any matter at all general and important. Afterwards one requires a great deal more skill to put oneself in the same condition one was in previously than one has to have to make great progress when one already has confirmed principles. In my case, if I have previously found some truths in the sciences (and I hope that the matters contained in this volume will make people conclude that I have found some), I can say that those are only the consequences of and dependent upon five or six major difficulties which I overcame and that I count these as so many battles in which victory was on my side.[1] Still, I will will not hesitate to state that I think I need to win only two or three others like those in order to reach the final goal of my project and that I am not so advanced in years that, given the ordinary course of nature, I still can have enough leisure to bring my project to its conclusion. But I think that I am all the more obliged to manage the time remaining to me, now that I have more hope of being able to use it well, and I would, no doubt, have many chances to lose that time, if I published the foundations of my physics. For although these foundations are almost all so evident that one need only hear them to believe them and there are none of them which, in my view, I cannot demonstrably prove, nevertheless, because it is impossible that they will agree with all the various opinions of other men, I anticipate being often distracted by the hostility they would give rise to.

One could say that this opposition would be useful, to the extent it makes me understand my mistakes and that, if I have anything good, others will by this means have a more complete understanding. Since several people can see more than one man by himself, if people begin from now on making use of my principles, they will also help me with their inventions. But even though I recognize that I am extremely prone to error and that I almost never have faith in the first thoughts which come to me, nevertheless the experience which I have of objections which people could make about

---

[1] The military language here, which offers us a sense of research as a series of battles against nature, is not an insignificant indication of the different attitude of the new science.

me prevents me from hoping for any benefit from such objections. For I have already undergone the criticism of so many of those whom I held as friends and of some others who I thought considered me indifferently and even of some in whom I knew malignity and envy would try hard enough to uncover what affection concealed from my friends. But it rarely happened that someone made an objection which I had not in some way anticipated, unless it was really distant from my subject, so that I have almost never met any critic of my opinions who did not appear to me to be less rigorous or less fair than myself. Moreover, I have never observed that anyone has discovered any truth of which people were previously ignorant by means of the disputes practised in the schools. For when each person tries to emerge victorious, people strive much harder to establish probability than to weigh the reasons on one side or the other, and those who have been good pleaders for a long time are not, on that account, better judges afterwards.

As for the practical use which other people derive from the communication of my thoughts, it could not be all that great, since I have not taken them so far that there is no need to add a great many things before they can be practically applied. And I think I can say without vanity that if there is anyone who can do that, this person should be me rather than anyone else, not because several minds incomparably better than mine could not be found in this world, but because one cannot conceive of something so well and make it one's own when one learns it from someone else as when one comes up with it oneself. What is really true about this material is that, although I have often explained some of my opinions to people with very good minds, who, while I was talking to them, seemed to understand my opinions very clearly, nonetheless, when they have repeated them, I have noticed that almost always they have changed them in such a way that I could no longer admit them as mine. Incidentally, I am more than happy to take the opportunity here to beg our descendants never to believe anything that people will tell them comes from me, when I never divulged them myself, and I am not astonished at the extravagant things which people attribute to those ancient philosophers whose writing we do not possess. I do not judge that their thoughts were really irrational on that account, seeing that they were the best minds of their times, but merely assume that their thoughts have been misrepresented to us. For we see also that it almost never happens that any of their disciples surpasses them, and I am confident that the most passionate of those people who follow Aristotle nowadays would consider themselves fortunate if they could have as much knowledge of nature as he had, even on condition that they would never know any more. They are like ivy which tends not to climb higher than the trees which support it and which often even comes down again when it has reached the tree tops. For it seems to me that those people also come back down, that is, make themselves in some way less knowledgeable than if they were to abandon their studying, when, not content with knowing everything intelligibly explained by their author, they wish to find, beyond that, the solution to several difficulties about which he has said nothing and has perhaps never even thought. However, their way of practising philosophy is extremely comfortable for those who have nothing but really mediocre minds, for the obscurity of the distinctions and the principles they use enables them to speak of everything as boldly as if they understood what they were talking about and to defend everything that they state against the most subtle and skillful minds, without anyone having the means to argue against them. In this it strikes me they are similar to a blind man who, in order to fight on equal terms against someone who can see, makes him come into the bottom of some really obscure cave. And I can state that such people have an interest in my abstaining from publishing the principles of philosophy I use, because, given that they are very simple and very evident, if I published them, I would be doing roughly the equivalent of opening some windows and bringing the light of day into this cave where they have gone down to fight each other. But even the best minds have no occasion to want to know these principles. For if they want to know how to speak about everything and to acquire the reputation of being scholarly, they will get there more easily in contenting themselves with probability which can be found in all sorts of matters without great trouble, rather than by seeking out the truth, which is not discovered except little by little in some matters and which, when it is a question of speaking of other matters, requires us to confess frankly that we are ignorant of them. If they would rather have the undoubtedly preferable condition of knowing a few truths over the vanity of appearing to be ignorant about nothing, and if they wish to follow a plan similar to my own, for that they do not need me to say anything more to them than I have already said in this discourse. For if they are capable of moving on further than I have done, they will also, with all the more reason, find for themselves everything I think I have found. Since I have never looked at anything except in due order, it is certain that what remains for me to discover is inherently more difficult and more hidden than what I have been able to find up to this point, and they would have much less pleasure in learning that from me than from themselves. Beyond that, the habit they will acquire by searching first for easy things and then moving on gradually by degrees to other more difficult things will serve them better than all my instructions will be able to. As for me, I am convinced that if I had been taught from my youth all the truths which I have found since my demonstrations and if I had had no trouble in learning them, I would perhaps have never known any others. At the very least I would never have acquired the habit and the skill which I think I have in constantly finding new truths to the extent that I apply myself in looking for them. In a word, if there is in the world some work which cannot be properly completed by anyone other than the same person who started it, it is the work I do.

It is true that so far the experiments which can help in that work are concerned, one man by himself is not sufficient to undertake them all. But he cannot put to practical use hands other than his own, except those of craftsmen or such people as he can pay, who with the hope of profit, which is a very effective means, will carry out everything exactly as he instructs them. As for volunteers who from curiosity or a desire to learn perhaps offer to help him, apart from the fact that ordinarily they promise more than they deliver and that they come up with nothing but fine propositions, none of which ever succeeds, they inevitably want to paid with the explanation of some difficulties or at least with compliments and useless discussions which would cost him more time than he could afford. As for the experiments which other people have already carried out, even though they should be willing enough to tell him about them, those who call such experiments secrets will never do that. Such experiments for the most part contain so many superfluous circumstances or ingredients that it would be very difficult for him to decipher the truth of them. Beyond that, he would find almost all of them badly explained or even false, because those who have carried them out have forced themselves to make the experiment appear to conform to their principles, so that if there were some experiments he could use, once again it would not be worth the time he would have to take up to pick them out. In the same way, if there were in the world someone in whom people had great confidence that he was capable of finding the greatest things and the most useful for the public as possible, and if for this reason other men tried hard to help him in every way to carry out his project with success, I do not see that they could do anything for him other than to furnish the costs of the experiments he needed to carry out, and, as to the rest, they could prevent his leisure from being taken away by anyone's importunity. But beyond the fact that I do not presume so much of myself as to wish to promise anything extraordinary and that I do not indulge in thoughts so vain as to imagine to myself that the pubic ought to show a great deal of interest in my plans, I do not have a soul so base that I would be willing to accept from anyone a favour which people might think I did not deserve.

All these considerations combined were the reason, three years ago, that I did not wish to publish the treatise which I had in my hands. I even made a resolution that during my life I would not make public any other treatise which was so general and from which one could learn the foundations of my physics. But, once again, there have been two other reasons since then which have obliged me to set down here some particular essays and to give the public some account of my actions and my plans. The first is that if I failed to do this, several people who knew of the intention I had previously of having some of my writing published could imagine that the reasons why I held back from doing so were more disadvantageous to me than they were. For although I do not like glory excessively, or, if I dare say it, although I dislike it to the extent that I see it as contrary to peace and quiet, which I value above everything, nonetheless I have also never tried to hide my actions as if they were crimes, nor have I taken many precautions to remain unknown, as much because I would have thought myself wrong if I did so, as because that would have given me a sort of unease which would, once again, have been contrary to the perfect peace of mind which I am looking for. Also, being always indifferently poised between care to get known or not to get known, since I could not prevent myself from acquiring some kind of reputation, I thought that I ought to do my best at least to avoid having a bad one. The other reason which obliged me to write this is that I realized more and more every day how the plan I had to teach myself was suffering a delay, because of an infinite number of experiments I needed and because it is impossible that I carry them out without the help of others. Although I do not flatter myself so much as to hope that the public pays great attention to my interests, nonetheless by the same token I do not want to let myself down so much that I give an excuse for those who will come after me to reproach me some day by saying that I could have left many things much better than I did, if I had not so neglected making them understand the ways in which they could contribute to my project.

And I thought that it would be easy for me to chose some matters which, without being subject to a great deal of controversy and without requiring me to state more of my principles than I wanted to, would permit me to reveal with sufficient clarity what I could or could not do in the sciences. In these matters I cannot say if I have been successful, and I have no desire to ward off anyone's criticism, as I talk in person about my own writings. But I will be very pleased if people examine them. In order for people to have more chances to do this, I request that all those who could have some objections take the trouble to send them to my publisher. If he tells me about them, I will try to attach my response to their objection and publish them at the same time. In this way, the readers, seeing the objections and my replies together, will judge the truth all the more easily. For I promise never to make long replies to such objections but only to confess my errors very candidly, if I recognize them, or else, if I cannot see them, to state simply what I believe is required for the defence of the things I have written, without adding there an explanation of any new material, so that I do not get endlessly involved with one matter after another. If some of those things which I have talked about at the beginning of *On Dioptrics* and *On Meteors* are shocking at first, because I call them suppositions and

I do not seem to have any desire to prove them, I urge people to have the patience to read the whole text with attention, and I hope that they will be satisfied with it. For it seems to me that the reasons follow there in sequence in such a way that the last ones are established by the first ones, which are their causes, and the first ones are reciprocally established by the last ones which are their effects. And people should not imagine that, in doing this, I am committing the error which logicians call arguing in a circle. For since experimentation makes most of these effects very certain, the causes which I have deduced do not serve so much to prove these effects as to explain them, so the case is precisely reversed: it is the causes which are proved by the effects.[1] And I used the name suppositions for these causes so that people might know that I think I can deduce them from these first truths which I have explained above but that I expressly wanted to avoid doing so, in order to prevent certain minds who imagine that they understand in a single day everything that another man has thought out in twenty years, as soon as he has said only two or three words about these matters to them, and who are all the more subject to error and less capable of truth, the more penetrating and bright they are, from taking the opportunity to construct some extravagant philosophy on what they believe are my principles, and in order to prevent people from attributing the fault for that to me. As for the opinions which are entirely mine, I do not seek to excuse them as new. To the extent that people think carefully about the reasons for them, I am confident that they will find my opinions so simple and so consistent with common sense that they will seem less extraordinary and less strange than some others which people might have on the same subjects. And, in addition, I do not boast that I am the first inventor of any of them, although I have never accepted them merely because they were said by others or because they have not been said by others, but simply because reason persuaded me to accept them.

If craftsmen cannot immediately carry out the inventions explained in the *Dioptrics*, I do not think that people can, for that reason, say that the text is a poor one. For to the extent that dexterity and skill are required to make and to adjust the machines which I have described, without missing the slightest detail, I would be no less amazed if they were successful on the first attempt than if someone could learn in a single day to play the lute extremely well, simply because someone had given him a good musi-

---

[1] Descartes here is identifying the process by which the new scientific method will proceed: an assumed cause, based on a theoretical understanding (like a mathematical model of the phenomenon under investigation), will hypothetically produce a certain effect. An experiment will then test to see if that effect does, in fact, occur. If it does, then there is a proof of the cause. If the effect does not occur, of course, then the assumed cause must be rejected. Experimental testing of predicted causes thus becomes the test of the theoretical cause.

cal score. And if I write in French, the language of my country, rather than in Latin, the language of my teachers, the reason is that I hope those who use only their natural reason, pure and simple, will judge my opinions better that those who believe nothing but ancient books. And as for those who combine good sense with study, who are the only ones I hope to have as my judges, I am confident that they will not be so partial to Latin that they will refuse to listen to my reasons because I explain them in the common language.

As for the rest, I do not wish to talk here in particular detail about the future progress which I hope to make in the sciences, nor to commit myself to promising the public what I am not confident of achieving. But I will only say that I have resolved not to use the time remaining to me for anything other than trying to acquire some knowledge of nature of such a kind that people can derive from it rules for medicine more reliable that those which they have at present, that my inclination keeps me so far away from all kinds of other projects, mainly those which can be practically useful to some people only by harming others, and that if some circumstance forced me to use my time in this way, I do not think I would be capable of succeeding in it. In saying this, I am making a declaration here which I well understand cannot make me important in the world, but also I have no desire to be important. I will always hold myself more obliged to those by whose favour I enjoy my leisure unencumbered than to those who might offer me the most prestigious positions on earth.

SOME BRIEF INTRODUCTORY COMMENTS ON DESCARTES' *DISCOURSE*

[The following is a slightly revised version of a lecture given to a class of Liberal Studies students in December 2005.]

If one were seeking to select one text from our Liberal Studies Great Books curriculum which first ushers in the modern age, one would have to consider René Descartes' *Discourse on Method*, published in 1637, a uniquely qualified selection. For in this relatively short work Descartes announces an agenda which marks a dramatic and decisive break with past traditions, lays down a project which became (and remains) the central concern of modern Western civilization, and, in the process, sets on the table the most important modern metaphor shaping our attempts to understand nature and ourselves. It is no accident that René Descartes has so often been hailed as the first and greatest modern thinker.

One should stress at the outset that, like all great revolutionary writers, Descartes is drawing extensively on the work of his contemporaries, particularly on Galileo (1564-1642), Harvey (1578-1657), and Bacon (1561-1626). But, unlike these well-known natural philosophers, Descartes is both a practising scientist and a first-rate philosopher. He is aware that whatever he has to offer by way of new explanations for natural phenomena must not merely make sense in itself and satisfy experimental testing but also must rest on a coherent method arising from a theory of how the human mind knows, from a theory of knowledge. That is, the new approach to natural science requires a rational justification. This philosophical basis of his scientific writing and the corollaries which arise from it give Descartes' text an enormous importance, over and above any new discoveries or theories he announces.

In this lecture I would like to review some of the more obvious ways in which Descartes' description and justification of his method do indeed mark a revolutionary moment in how we have come to understand what knowledge is and how we acquire and evaluate it. Most of these points are obvious enough from Descartes' text, but, as his heirs, who have been raised to believe in his program and to dedicate our energies to it, we may not fully grasp just how decisive a turn he is inviting his contemporaries to take.

But first an important caveat. It is really important to understand that in the early 17th century there was no clear sense of what the "new" science (or natural philosophy) should or could be. There was not then, as there is now, a general consensus about anything one might call a scientific method or any agreed-upon way to evaluate claims made on the basis of experiments or bold new mathematically-based hypotheses. Nor was it clear where or whether one could draw a clear line separating natural philosophy from astrology or alchemy or magic. Thus, while there was certainly a sense of revolutionary change in the air, a desire to break with past authorities, and a growing interest in new ways of looking at natural phenomena, especially with the aid of new machines (telescopes, air pumps, and later microscopes), natural scientists were still in the process of trying to establish and agree about just what their activities involved.

Before reviewing some of the major points Descartes makes, we might first notice the tone of the book, a particularly interesting feature of the argument. Unlike Galileo's frequently satirical voice or Bacon's polemical prose, Descartes strives from the start to reassure us—he is offering, he says, not a blueprint we should all follow, but merely his own personal story; he has no desire for fame nor any radical agenda, especially in any matters which affect his firm religious faith; he is not challenging any important social customs or political arrangements; he is not even sure he wants to write or publish this book; and so on. There is a deliberate sense here of a self-effacing, modest, calm, reasonable, and co-operative personality, something very much at odds with the bold and challenging ideas he is setting out in rapid succession.

Of course, this tone is something of a rhetorical ploy. But we should not therefore dismiss it out of hand as a hypocritical Trojan Horse strategy intended merely to deceive suspicious authorities. For there is no reason to suppose that Descartes is not being perfectly sincere when he affirms his Christian faith or informs us of his intense distaste for personal or political squabbling and his preference for peace and quiet above everything else or proposes a radical scientific hypothesis as a thought experiment rather than the truth of things. Naturally, with the example of Galileo to ponder (as he reminds us), Descartes is well aware of one possible response to what he is proposing, but that does not entitle us to claim (as students sometimes seem fond of doing) that his modest candour is simply a sham. In one respect, of course, Descartes' very calm personal tone plays an important part in the argument, since (as we shall see) one of the most distinctive features of what he is proposing is that his method is (he says) something anyone can practise. The book may be his own personal story, but there is an obvious invitation here for others who find what he says agreeable to follow his lead. His decision to write the *Discourse* in French rather than in Latin, the language of the scholars, seems clearly a part of his intention to reassure people about what he is doing and to encourage them to agree with him and to assist his work.

In some ways, the most devastating aspect of Descartes' argument comes right at the start in the friendly low-key account he provides of his own education. For he makes it clear early on that he is radically dissatisfied with the excellent but conventional education he has received, because it has not answered his desire for truth. He has experienced a thorough immersion in the received wisdom of the ages and the accepted ways of understanding literature, nature, morality, history, and philosophy, but he wants something none of those disciplines apparently can offer, an assurance of certainty. At the core of his project lies his demand for knowledge which is not subject to disputes or probabilities. Hence, his polite but firm rejection of everything he has been taught.

In making this demand, Descartes is taking issue with the opinions of most of his contemporaries. Many of them continue, some with increasing zealotry, to assert the traditional claims to the truth established by religion and by the long tradition of linking an understanding of nature with divine purposes. Many others, however, including very well educated and reasonable people, have, after more than a century of bloody wars over religious questions, abandoned the notion that such certainty is available in any of the major questions of life and have sought refuge in scepticism or in the developing science of probability. If we live in a world of competing truths and are killing each other over rival interpretations of scripture, we might as well give up a search for Truth (with a capital T) and live quietly, organizing our lives in accordance with the customs of the people around us, the position recommended by Montaigne (1533-1592), or we must seek out and follow what, as best we can ascertain, is most probably true or the course of action which has a better chance of leading to success (a position most famously publicized by Pascal's Wager, which appeared some years after the *Discourse*: since God either exists and punishes those who disbelieve and rewards those who believe in Him or else He does not exist and there is no afterlife of rewards and punishment, the reasonable person will believe, since he has a lot more to lose from disbelief than from belief).[1]

Descartes' method, then, begins with his rejection of these common ways of thinking about the truth.[2] He will adopt a sceptical attitude towards

---

[1]There is not space here to discuss in any detail the wider social context surrounding the development of the new science, but it is important to note that the century of extraordinarily brutal and prolonged and inconclusive religious warfare following Luther's Reformation had, in effect, destroyed the traditional framework of belief which enabled Europeans to share a common way of understanding the world. For many thinkers, the new science offered the hope of a language which could transcend religious differences and which would enable people of very different faiths to agree without interminable and bloody arguments about scripture.

[2]This statement is not entirely true, of course, because Descartes repeatedly informs us of his faith in his Roman Catholic religion and his deference to its authority. However, since the truth of that religion, in his view, is not established by human reason and since he himself is not qualified to be a prophet, it is not part of his project.

everything he has learned and everything he can perceive with his senses, until such time as he can with his own reasoning satisfy himself of some basic truths, and he will adopt the customs of the people he lives among, but not with a view to remaining in that state. For he is confident that from this temporary vantage point he can construct something much firmer if he simply looks for it in a new place, namely within himself, within the framework of his own ability to think reasonably and to come to unassailable conclusions about particular things.

In setting up this new method, for all his cautionary words about how it might not suit everyone, Descartes is, in fact, making clear that anyone capable of rational thought will be able, not merely to understand him, but also to follow in his footsteps. His opening comments about the average quality of his own mind are not just false modesty but an important claim for what is to follow. He is thus suggesting two very new features of his method, apart from the fact that it does not require any deference to or, for that matter, knowledge of the traditional ways of understanding the world: it is egalitarian, requiring no more reason than most intelligent people possess, and it is self-correcting and progressive, for errors can be dealt with by a better application of the method, and later thinkers can build on the work of earlier ones (false results come from mistakes in applying the method, not from any inherent limitations in the human mind attributable to original sin). Hence, disputes will be capable of resolution, without the need for interminable arguments about the most basic things, of the sort common to interpretations of Aristotle, for example, or to scholarly disputes about ancient texts, in which nothing is ever finally resolved. Such discussions, Descartes points out, may establish a scholar's reputation for learning and make him famous and rich, but they leave us where we always were, in a state of uncertainty. His method, he is confident, will lead to a progressive improvement in what we know.

Descartes is, of course, best known for his celebrated reflections on what there might be which he can know with certainty, once he has rejected all he has been taught and all sense experience, and for his first important conclusion: "I think; therefore, I am" (although to describe more accurately what Descartes means, we should probably translate that famous sentence as "I am thinking; therefore, I am," since the assurance of one's own existence comes only while the thinking is going on). Hence, while he is capable of doubting or being deceived about nature around him (including his own body), he has something within him, the "I", which he identifies with the soul, the existence of which is for him absolutely certain, because, even in the process of doubting everything, he cannot deny that he is thinking.

In reviewing Descartes' description of these first steps in his reflections, we should remember that what he offers in the *Discourse* is merely a rapid summary sketch of the argument he presents in much more detail in the *Meditations on First Philosophy*, published some years later. So those who are tempted to make quick objections should first direct their attention to the later book.[1] What matters here is not so much the philosophical adequacy of the argument but rather the direct effects his reasoning has for an understanding of nature and of the method most appropriate for expanding what we know. That said, however, one needs to pay attention to the steps Descartes goes through, because these give a definite shape to the method he is proposing and lead to certain major consequences.

In discussing that famous first conclusion, Descartes establishes his most important criterion for accepting something as true:

> After that, I considered in general what is necessary for a proposition to be true and certain, for since I had just found one idea which I knew to be true and certain, I thought that I ought also to understand what this certitude consisted of. And having noticed that in the sentence "I think; therefore, I am" there is nothing at all to assure me that I am speaking the truth, other than that I see very clearly that in order to think it is necessary to exist, I judged that I could take as a general rule the point that the things which we conceive very clearly and very distinctly are all true.

But what, one might ask at once, does he mean by that key phrase "conceive very clearly and very distinctly"? If those are the qualities a thing must possess for it to be true, we need to understand just what they are. About this point there has been much discussion, but in the context of the *Discourse* the words seem to refer to an axiomatic intuitive certainty, of the sort we encounter most frequently, as Descartes reminds us, in mathematics, truths which are self-evident and do not admit of reasonable disagreement (like, for example, the claim that things equal to the same thing are equal to each other) and other truths which we can deduce from these.

Descartes then, very quickly and cursorily, faces up to a major corner he seems to have painted himself into. How is he to have any reliable knowl-

---

[1] One can raise some immediate objections, in particular about Descartes' identifying the "I" in "I think" as a permanent reality and in equating it to the human soul when it may be, as Nietzsche suggests, simply an accident of French grammar. However, in the *Discourse*, Descartes is not setting out the more detailed argument he offers in his much more philosophically interesting book, *Meditations on First Philosophy*. In reading the argument in the *Meditations*, one should pay particular attention to the Objections made by a number of well known thinkers whom Descartes invited to respond to his case and to his replies to them.

edge of the external world, when all his senses are deceptive and the only truth is his own inner process of thinking? How can his knowledge escape total self-consciousness, a thoroughgoing solipsism? The argument (or rather the summary sketch of the later argument) concerning God is the key stage which enables him to take this step.

It is not uncommon for first-time readers of the *Discourse* to find this section rather problematic and to offer the comment that Descartes is here simply placating religious authorities rather than being sincere in his affirmations of belief. Whatever the nature of Descartes' religious beliefs (and there seems little evidence that his statements about them are not sincere), it is important to note that the paragraphs about God are an essential part of the philosophical argument, a necessary logical foundation for the method he is proposing. Without them, the certainty he is seeking would not be available.

The argument for the existence of God is, in part, a traditional one, as Descartes acknowledges. Since he has ideas of perfection and of all the flawless qualities of God, he questions where these ideas might have arisen. As a limited and imperfect human being, he does not have those qualities himself. And they cannot have come from sense experience of nature or from outside natural sources, all of which he has discounted. Hence, the idea of such qualities must have come from somewhere else, from some being that manifests these qualities and is of a higher order of goodness than himself, that is, from God. The existence of God is thus necessarily true.

The perfection of God then enables Descartes to establish the validity of his principle that what we perceive clearly and distinctly must be true, for

> . . . the very principle which I have so often taken as a rule—only to recognize as true all those things which we conceive very clearly and very distinctly—is guaranteed only because of the fact that God is or exists, that He is a perfect being, and that everything which is in us comes from Him. From that it follows that our ideas or notions, being real things which come from God, to the extent that they are clear and distinct, in that respect cannot be anything but true.

Hence, the truth of the clear and distinct ideas we can formulate about the world are underwritten by the existence of a perfect Deity.

To some people this may look suspiciously like circular reasoning: the existence of God is established by the clarity and distinctness of Descartes' perception of His perfection, and then the perfection of God guarantees the truth of ideas which Descartes perceives clearly and distinctly. However, as I mentioned before, we are being given here merely a summary sketch of the argument, and so if we do have such reservations, we should direct our attention to the case Descartes makes in the *Meditations*. For our purposes what matters here are some of the more obvious effects of this line of reasoning. Given what Descartes has said up to this point, certain very revolutionary consequences follow for anyone interested in exploring human knowledge and sorting out what we can and do know from what we are uncertain of.

First, according to Descartes' line of reasoning, the world is radically dualistic. The spiritual, knowing world of the "I," the human soul, is set over against the mechanical world of nature, including the human body and all non-human animals, which is without any spiritual dimension. The latter operates as a clock. And we understand it, as we do a clock, by using our minds to analyze its parts bit by bit, building our knowledge from simple ideas we are sure about into more complex systems of knowledge, like the development of geometric theorems. It is worth noting that Descartes is fully aware that there must be some interaction between the soul and the body, since what we think has an effect on how we act. Hence, his later remarks about how the soul is more than a pilot on a ship for "it is necessary that the soul is joined and united more closely with the body, so that it has, in addition, feelings and appetites similar to ours and thus makes up a true human being." But he has little to offer by way of suggesting how that interaction might take place (elsewhere he locates the place where the soul and the body interact in the pineal gland, because he can find no other use for it). This matter remains a highly contentious matter today, what has come to be called "the problem of consciousness," especially for those, like Richard Dawkins, who wish to understand all human experience as the result of physical processes.

This metaphor obviously encourages a particular relationship between human beings and nature, giving the knowing mind a pre-eminent position and charging it with the responsibility for finding out about nature. Gone is traditional sense of human beings as privileged participants in nature, with responsibilities for respecting nature either as divine (the classical pagan view) or as a uniquely mysterious creation by God (the traditional Christian view). Descartes' picture of nature as an unthinking machine provides a license for human beings to probe, explore, experiment— in a word, to tamper with—nature in the search for knowledge, without having to worry about any spiritual qualities in the objects under investigation, because everything outside the human soul operates like a machine. This metaphor, more than anything else, accounts for the astonishingly aggressive attitude Western science quickly developed and has maintained towards nature.[1]

Later in the *Discourse* the driving motivation for this way of thinking emerges. Descartes wants his method to give us, not merely an understanding of nature, but power over it, something that will make us "as it were, the masters and possessors of nature." Like Francis Bacon, Descartes wishes to transform the purpose of natural science into something immediately practical, a form of knowledge which people can use effectively to attack and alter nature to suit human needs, especially in medicine.

Traditionally, of course, the major purpose of natural philosophy, both among the Greeks and the Medieval Christians, was to encourage contemplation. It was, if you like, a form of spiritual discipline or celebration which encouraged in the enquirer a sense of higher moral purpose in the world around us. The very idea of altering nature to fit human desires or seeking to control nature was absurd or impious. For Descartes and Bacon, this traditional emphasis produced no useful results, nothing which might improve the conditions human beings had to face. A constant preoccupation with the moral purposes of creation produced, in their view, a sterile, unproductive, and disputatious form of knowledge. By setting such concerns to one side and focusing on nature as a soulless machine whose efficient causes human beings could understand, control, and use, the new science would acquire the knowledge necessary to transform the world for the better.

Descartes is here urging something extremely familiar to us, something we take for granted as a major imperative of our culture. But it was by no means so obvious to his contemporaries, especially those who (like many pious scholars antagonistic to Galileo's work) were primarily concerned about what might happen to human life once the importance of the moral framework of the universe was set aside in the quest for efficient power over nature.[2]

This is not to deny that many modern natural scientists from Descartes' day to the present have been motivated primarily by the wonders of nature, engage in their scientific speculation out of a sense of intense curiosity, and derive contemplative satisfaction from their work. But it is no less

[1]That aggressive attitude emerges most clearly when Descartes talks of his investigations into nature using the language of military campaigns.

[2]We still manifest this old objection when we express reservations about the unchecked development in some areas, especially in the science of human reproduction (cloning, stem cells, and so on), all of which is an energetic continuation of Descartes' project. To raise moral objections to such work is to echo many of the complaints of traditionalists worried about the shift in emphasis brought about by the new science.

true that the major imperative to carry on science so intensely in schools and the research establishments has increasingly become the desire to gain more power over nature, even at the expense of that wonder. Many writers have acknowledged that the modern project launched by Descartes and others has, in fact, gradually emptied the world of wonder, for we have so many reasonable explanations for natural phenomena and have placed so much of nature directly under our own control (or, more accurately, perhaps, we think we have), that we are seldom personally confronted with nature as a mysterious presence, and when we are, we often do not know how to react.

What Descartes is proposing here also has important consequences for the vital role mathematics must play in our understanding of nature. For the clarity and directness which, thanks to God, reveal the truth to us are, above all, conveyed in mathematical deductions. Hence, this *Discourse* launches the strong demand that modern science must follow mathematic logic, and the truth of its claims emerges from the mathematic foundations upon which those are based. Science, in other words, needs to rely upon equations rather than verses cited from scripture or traditional interpretations of Aristotle. This emphasis is significantly different from early 17th century science in England, where, under the energetic leadership of Francis Bacon, the stress is much more on experimental evidence, the collection of observed facts, and the inductions one might draw from repeated observation and testing. And for some time, there was a lively dispute between English science (based on experiments) and Continental science (based on mathematics). In fact, however, one should not overemphasize these differences. Descartes makes clear in the *Discourse* how important experiments are, and Bacon repeatedly called attention to the imperfections of sense experience (all the more evident when frequently defective machinery was involved, like imperfect lenses in telescopes and leaky air pumps). The major synthesis between the two approaches to natural science occurred in the work of Isaac Newton (1643-1727), whose work combined mathematically-based hypotheses with key experiments to test the explanatory power of the equations.

Once he has established the basis of his method, Descartes then quickly offers a summary list of what he turned his attention to, the natural phenomena which he feels his method has enabled him to understand. In the midst of this section, he puts on the table an idea which was later to have the most revolutionary implications for our understanding of nature and ourselves, that is, a historical approach to understanding nature scientifically. It is worth having a close look at this suggestion, particularly for anyone who is going on to follow what later thinkers will do with what at this stage is little more than a tentative hypothesis.

What if, Descartes suggests,

> God now created somewhere in imaginary space enough material to
> compose [a new world], and if He set in motion, in a varied and dis-
> orderly way, the various parts of this material, so that it created a
> chaos as confused as poets could make it, and then afterwards He did
> nothing other than lend His ordinary help to nature and allow it to
> act according to the laws which He established.

What if, in other words, we were to seek to understand the world as something with a unique history, a series of different stages through which it
passed, under the guidance of divinely ordained natural laws, from disor-
ganized materials into the ordered structure we see all around us? This is,
for Descartes, an extremely bold and potentially dangerous idea. For at the
centre of a Christian understanding of nature had long been the insis-
tence, based on scripture, that God made the world and everything in it in
its present state at the time of Creation. Hence, the earth does not have a
history, not in the sense of a unique linear development out of something
very different from what it is now. Descartes' hypothetical proposal suggests that the only permanent things are the laws God established to allow
nature to act as He wants it to through various stages and that we can
come to a useful understanding of what is in the world by seeing it as
something with a long history of change.

The second doctrinal problem this suggestion has always run into is that it
imposes restrictions on God. If matter always obeys the laws God has established to guide its development, then He is not free to intervene in unexpected and miraculous ways. God is, in effect, the servant of His own
laws, not totally free. This point has always been the major objection of
Christian thinkers to the often popular view called Deism (which corre-
sponds roughly with what Descartes is proposing: God created the original
matter, established the natural laws governing its development, and does
not intervene).

Newton's opposition to this view of the world is well known. For him, God
established the universe in its present form, and the only possible changes
came from unexpected "miraculous" divine interventions. Nonetheless,
within a century of Newton's great work, natural scientists (including Im-
manuel Kant) were writing accounts of the historical development of the
earth and of the universe itself.

The dangers in this approach stem not merely from its challenge to ortho-
dox belief. Any historically based understanding of the world carries a la-
tent political message, as well, namely that the existing state of things is
not something permanently ordained but rather the result of a historical
process (which, presumably, is still going on). Hence, a historical ap-